P9-CLO-826

SEEING

TOMORROW

SEEING
TOMORROW

Rewriting the Rules of Risk

RON S. DEMBO
ANDREW FREEMAN

JOHN WILEY & SONS, INC.

New York • Chichester • Weinheim • Brisbane • Singapore • Toronto

This book is printed on acid-free paper. ∞

Copyright © 1998 by Ron S. Dembo and Andrew Freeman. All rights reserved.

Published by John Wiley & Sons, Inc.

No part of this publication may be reproduced, stored in a retrieval system or transmitted in any form or by any means, electronic, mechanical, photocopying, recording, scanning or otherwise, except as permitted under Section 107 or 108 of the 1976 United States Copyright Act, without either the prior written permission of the Publisher, or authorization through payment of the appropriate per-copy fee to the Copyright Clearance Center, 222 Rosewood Drive, Danvers, MA 01923, (978) 750-8400, fax (978) 750-4744. Requests to the Publisher for permission should be addressed to the Permissions Department, John Wiley & Sons, Inc., 605 Third Avenue, New York, NY 10158-0012, (212) 850-6011, fax (212) 850-6008, E-Mail: PERMREQ@WILEY.COM.

This publication is designed to provide accurate and authoritative information in regard to the subject matter covered. It is sold with the understanding that the publisher is not engaged in rendering legal, accounting, or other professional services. If legal advice or other expert assistance is required, the services of a competent professional person should be sought.

Library of Congress Cataloging-in-Publication Data:

Dembo, R. S. (Ron S.)
    Seeing tomorrow : rewriting the rules of risk / Ron S. Dembo,
Andrew Freeman.
       p. cm.
    Includes index.
    ISBN 0-471-24736-7 (alk. paper)
    1. Investments. 2. Risk management. 3. Speculation.
I. Freeman, Andrew. II. Title.
HG4521.D485 1998
332.6—dc21   97-49920

Printed in the United States of America.

10 9 8 7 6 5 4 3 2 1

For Alyson and Hazel

ACKNOWLEDGMENTS

This book is the product of a true collaboration. Andrew Freeman met Ron S. Dembo in 1995, when he was researching an article on risk for *The Economist*. He visited the offices of Algorithmics Inc., in Toronto, expecting to hear typical corporate PR. Instead, he was swept into a whirlwind conversation about Risk and Regret—concepts that had long preoccupied Dr. Dembo and formed the intellectual basis of his software business. Intrigued, the journalist and the academic-turned-entrepreneur debated whether they should try to write, together, a work that described new ideas about the way we all make decisions involving risk. Much cogitating and many late nights ensued. Ideas were swapped by telephone, e-mail, and fax, and even in posted letters, as the project grew in scope. The result is *Seeing Tomorrow*.

We must thank many people. Ron Layard-Liesching of Pareto Partners first suggested that we might like each other, and then added that we should meet anyway. Over the years, plenty of individuals have given generously of their time and ideas in the pursuit of good reporting and sound thinking. Charles Sanford of Bankers Trust and Stephen Ross of Yale University deserve special mention. Meir

Statman of Santa Clara University was especially helpful on behavioral finance. Peter Bernstein, who wrote a brilliant book on risk, inspired us to believe that there is widespread interest in the subject. Jacqui Dunal, of Algorithmics Inc., was a selfless and enthusiastic contributor to the preparation of a legible manuscript, as well as an essential anchor when the authors were at different ends of the earth. We gratefully acknowledge the help and insights of several others who read the manuscript at an early stage. We remain responsible for any errors that have survived.

The central ideas behind *Seeing Tomorrow* owe much to years of hard work and advocacy by Ron S. Dembo. His ideas on measuring risk, although in print for many years in technical papers, presentations, and a patent, have heretofore not been available to the general public. Employees at Algorithmics Inc. have been invaluable as colleagues and as critics. Special thanks to Michael Zerbs, Michael Durland, Andrew Aziz, Dan Rosen, and David Penny. The many hours spent debating the central ideas of this book with them have contributed to the theory.

Andrew Freeman owes much to his colleagues at *The Economist* and, before that, the *Financial Times*. Special thanks are due to Bill Emmott, the editor of *The Economist*, and to Clive Crook, its deputy editor, for permission to draw on some previously published articles, including a fine and relevant piece on decision theory by Mr. Crook. Merril Stevenson was an inspiring finance editor as well as a wonderful colleague who passed on the art of making complex ideas into understandable statements.

Thanks to our agent, Beverley Slopen, for proving that there can be an Upside in book writing. Myles Thompson at John Wiley & Sons, Inc., has been a supportive and enthusiastic editor who needed remarkably little prodding to see the potential merits of our work. Maryan Malone of Publications Development Company was an insightful and helpful editor of the text.

Thanks to our children—Justine and Ella Dembo, and Luke, Max, and Georgia Freeman-Mills—who generously gave up precious time with their fathers so that this book could be written.

Our biggest thanks we offer to our wives, Alyson Hannas and Hazel Mills. They saw firsthand the perils of book writing. They tolerated the daydreams and absences that characterized the progress of ideas into prose, though they joked occasionally that the real spousal pair in this group was the two authors. Without their support, sometimes maintained in trying circumstances, neither of us could have finished this book. It is dedicated to them.

Ron S. Dembo
Andrew Freeman

CONTENTS

xi

Introduction

IT REALLY HAPPENED

I magine for a moment that it is late 1994 and you are George Soros, one of the world's best-known investors. In keeping with your lofty status and your desire to diversify your investments, you have formed a joint venture with Paul Reichmann, one of the world's best-known property developers. The combination of your resources is staggering: between the two of you, skylines in several major cities have been reshaped, and governments have been brought to their knees. In this latest coup, you stand together on the brink of a huge deal in fast-emerging Mexico that will add hundreds of millions to your already substantial fortunes. At the last minute, however, there is a hitch. Your prospective local partner in the deal wants better terms, to reflect some turbulence in currency markets. The Mexican peso has suddenly fallen and could fall further. Will you agree to change the contract by 10 percent in your local partner's favor? How should you approach this decision? Do you lock in a sure thing today? Or do you wait, hoping that things will improve so that your returns become even better? Do you concede or do you play hardball?

Two of the world's shrewdest business brains, George Soros and Paul Reichmann, got this deal completely and horribly wrong—so much so, it fell apart. To their dismay, they never did gain the prime site in Mexico City that they had hoped to develop. The full story is an object lesson in how not to make decisions about risk (see Chapter 1). These titans went wrong because they made a classic error in thinking about their decision: they failed to take into account the possibility that things could go from bad to worse. They underestimated the Regret that they would feel if the deal failed altogether.

Big players are not alone in making such mistakes. Average people may think in different terms, but they regularly face decisions about risk that can have a huge impact on their lives. Most readers probably know someone who lost everything in the housing market at some point in the past fifteen years. In London, New York, and Toronto, house prices have swung up and down with alarming speed. A safe equity cushion one day has become a yawning "negative equity" debt the next. Today's expensive and desirable studio apartment can become tomorrow's unsalable and poky white elephant. Even as this book was in preparation, one of the authors, who sold a house in 1994, watched in dismay as property prices in England defied expectations and rose to new heights. (In Chapter 6, we offer some telling examples of just how poor the thinking about house price risk can be.)

The truth is, calamities do happen. Sometimes, as was the case with Mexico in 1994, the reverberations are felt throughout the world's financial markets and economies. Such events make palpable what we know to be true in theory but, like George Soros and Paul Reichmann, too often overlook or choose to ignore in practice. Risk lies ahead of us, not in the past. It is no use looking over our shoulder and assuming that we can find there all we need to know. In that stance, we will never see the vehicles that are bearing down on us. (Mexico's apparently stable exchange rate fooled almost everyone.) Yet, looking over our shoulder is precisely what most of us do, in business and in our personal lives. How many of us have metaphorically kicked ourselves for wrong decisions that seem obvious and easy in retrospect? Chances are that we were guilty of poor thinking, a.k.a. past thinking.

For centuries, mathematicians, economists, and philosophers have sought ways to model how we make choices. Our behavior is governed by many things—our tastes, our budget, and our appetite for risk, to name a few. Our measurement and management of financial risk are based on our ability to relate some central ideas. What is our risk exposure? Can we do things that will limit our risk? Are there potential controls that will protect us against suffering excessive loss? We all face risk decisions. Daily, we must make decisions that involve financial risks:

- Should we buy a house now?
- Should we invest in the stock our broker is suggesting?
- Should we pay the seemingly high charge for per-diem car rental insurance during a vacation? Should we take a $1,000 deductible and pay $800, or a $50 deductible and pay $3,000 for insurance on the car we own?
- Should we set aside a college tuition fund now, for our three-year-old daughter?
- Should we start a pension plan and, if so, how much should we set aside?
- Should we undergo an experimental medical procedure that might cure us of a long-standing illness?
- Should we refinance our mortgage now, or later?
- Should we buy a lottery ticket?
- Should we go on strike and risk losing our job?
- Should we, as owners, refuse a wage-increase demand and risk a strike that might destroy our business?

As we face and make many of these decisions, we will occasionally Regret our choices.

Individuals are not unique in facing such decisions. Financial institutions—banks, brokers, and insurers—are nothing more than risk traders who buy one risk and sell another. Their business is based on profit from risk, and they are barraged with opportunities for risk taking. In recent years, as financial markets have become dramatically more complex, these institutions have had to develop innovative ways of controlling their risk exposures. But it is inherently difficult for these banks, investment firms, and insurance companies to understand the extent of the risks they are assuming at any given moment. Their ability to understand risk often lags seriously behind their urgent need to do so.

What guides people when they must make a decision in a financially risky setting? Why do different people place differing amounts on the same bet? Why do some people have larger exposure to mutual funds than others? Why do people change their strategy as the stakes change in a game? How do people measure risk? On what basis do they decide whether to accept a risky bet? Why do they buy lottery tickets or insurance policies even when the odds are against them? How should banks measure and control risk so that the financial system remains healthy?

There are no simple answers to these questions. However, in our increasingly complex world, we are forced to make decisions that, more and more, involve understanding and systematic assessment of these and other risks. Just think of how much more choice and complexity we encounter compared to our parents. How many options did they have to choose from when mortgaging their house, choosing life insurance, or investing? Mutual funds, or such exotic instruments as exchange-traded options, were scarcely available a generation ago. No one had yet dreamed of mortgage-backed securities. It was almost impossible to buy exposure to foreign markets. Today, these all exist; tomorrow the choices will multiply. So what are we to do? It is no longer good enough to operate on intuition alone. We require tools to help us quantify the options we face.

We have written this book because we think it is time to rewrite the rules on risk. Too many mistakes have resulted from outmoded and flawed approaches to its definition and management. Strangely, most people seem to have given up asking simple questions about risk.

It is true that some progress has been made in quantifying and measuring risk. Huge markets now exist in financial instruments known as derivatives, which are designed to lay off or assume risks of various kinds. Individual investors now take for granted information about their investments that was once unavailable or reserved for large institutions. But we believe that most of the methods available and in use today are inadequate for analyzing the types of risks that investors face.

In some respects, people are far more aware of the problem than they used to be. Masses of consumers have shifted their savings from low-paying bank accounts into money market accounts or more aggressive mutual funds. They have been actively assuming risk in exchange for greater returns on their cash. And people purchasing insurance can make much more finely calibrated decisions about how much risk they wish to anticipate (as we will see, this market remains frustratingly slow at developing useful new policies).

Yet much of this increased awareness and embracing of risk has been accompanied by a collective shrug of shoulders. People know they are exposed to more risk, but that's OK; nothing terrible will happen. In contrast, we think that many of the everyday ways in which we are exposed to risk are mistakenly overlooked. Moreover, they share common elements with the more formal risk disciplines that are associated with financial markets and banking.

Holding an investment or a portfolio of investments is like taking a gamble. At the end of the race (which could be tonight, next week, or years hence), we will either win or lose. Yet, as we all know, when we place a bet we are faced with a single, unique decision that will probably not be repeated or will only be repeated a few times. We need to make that decision despite the uncertainty the future brings, and we need to make it *now*.

We will show that many bankruptcies, bad deals, and large losses come about because scenarios under which we might lose in a big way were never considered. A few people, it is true, adopt a structured approach to decisions that involve risk. They literally map out their options and assess the pros and cons implied by each one. Many more people tend to act intuitively. "Go with your gut" is a common approach, and, as often as it succeeds, it produces horrendous results that leave people in unhappy circumstances. It is revealing to analyze some of that intuitive process. By doing so, we can gain new insights into the role risk plays in our everyday lives.

Although questions about risk permeate our daily activities, many of our existing views of risk are too narrow and too formal. In fact, our knowledge about risk is still in its infancy. We lack accepted definitions and agreed-on ways of measuring risk. In particular, we too often assume that what has happened in the past will prove a reliable guide to the future. In the following pages, we will describe a number of concepts that will change all that. Some of these are the result of years of research by Ron Dembo. Through Algorithmics, his software firm, he has shown that apparently abstract ideas can have practical and powerful applications in the real world. Moreover, the framework set out in this book is no different from the one Algorithmics uses to help the world's most sophisticated banks manage their risks.

The central concept we introduce is Regret—the neglected "R" behind Risk and Return. As we will see, Regret is a common enough idea in several branches of academic economics and finance. But its applicability to risk management has been almost entirely missed. We hope to show that Regret is a powerful tool for aligning how we intuitively judge risks with the more formal methods that we use for quantifying them.

But our purpose is far broader and more ambitious than this single concept. We hope to set out a convincing new way of thinking about risk, beginning with identifying the basic building blocks and then using them to construct a firm structure for risk management and risk-adjusted performance measurement. In the following chapters, we show ways of visualizing risk that help to explain the new rules. We also make a few calculations to illustrate how risk measures work in practice. No one should be put off by the math involved. Where possible, we use words to augment and explain our use of symbols. Most mathematicians confess that they sometimes struggle with symbols; they must read and then slowly reread a proof of a theorem before they can be satisfied that it is correct. The process is not unlike reading a recipe several times before we relate the instructions to the ingredients that are needed to make a dish. Only the best chefs can hold an entire menu's recipes in their heads. For any reader who feels "stuck" or confused by a passage, we have simple advice: Don't be afraid to read it again!

None of us can afford to ignore risk; it is always present in our lives, and all of us need a better framework for understanding and managing it. We offer the framework described in these pages as a step in the right direction. We think that it captures, much more than others, how we as individuals actually think about risk. Our framework is built around our view of the future, not modeled solely on the past. And it is adaptable enough to allow each of us to express our own forward-looking attitudes and fears, rather than relying on an assumption that other people share broadly similar views. Unlike some commonly used numerical and statistical measures of risk, our framework is also closely aligned to our intuitions about how we feel when we eye one risk relative to another. Finally, we suggest that our approach allows a consistent view of risk. It is coherent whether it relates to a single investment or an entire portfolio. Where other measures of risk break down or are manifestly inadequate, we suggest new and powerful ways of approaching the subject.

We take inspiration from the picture that so dramatically graces the cover of this book. Painted by Caspar David Friedrich around 1818, this highly Romantic image is called "Wanderer above a Sea of Fog" — an apt metaphor for how we face the future and the risks it will bring. If, like the subject in the painting, we look forward, the landscape is wild, indistinct, and hazy, as if obscured by fog. We can see vague outlines; occasional flashes of detail emerge, such as the trees that are startlingly clear along some of the rocky outcrops. How should we travel in this mysterious landscape? From our vantage point, we can imagine different possible paths, but each is foggy, perhaps containing perils and travails. How can we navigate in such a world? Without seeing what tomorrow will bring, how we can manage our affairs with sufficient confidence today?

The effort to see tomorrow has ancient precedent. Raymond DeVoe, a stockbroker who writes a wry newsletter replete with history, points out that the Romans gave us the word "speculator," derived from *specula*, a watchtower of the kind that ringed imperial Rome at strategic intervals and from which approaching danger could be spotted. By the apogee of the Roman Empire, the watchtowers stretched for thousands of miles, acting as an early warning system that allowed the swift dispatch of legions to wherever trouble was brewing. Thus, a pure definition of a speculator is: someone who tries to see dangers in the future and act upon them. Only more recently did the word "speculator" acquire a pejorative edge in financial markets! DeVoe also reminds us that Friedrich was not the only artist who has captured the sense of peering into the unknown. Frederick Remington painted a dramatic and famous picture called "Friend or Foe?" It shows an Indian brave on his horse atop a cliff. Amid poor light and swirling snow, he is focusing on a distant line of riders in the valley below. Whether they represent a threat or are returning friends is impossible to tell.

In one fundamental respect, decisions involving financial risk are different from other decisions that we face in life. Whereas many facets of daily life shift with glacial, almost predictable, slowness, financial markets can change in the blink of an eye. Think about it. Let's say you wish to hire a carpenter to build some shelves. In this case, you can be pretty confident that the carpenter who was excellent six months earlier will still be at the top of his trade. In other words, history is an excellent guide. It is unlikely that someone who was very good then will be incompetent now.

Contrast this with finance. A brilliant fund manager can lose everything in a matter of days. Sometimes mere minutes can send a high-flying company's shares into free fall. History is no guide, or at best a guide that can be dangerously misleading. So rapidly can things change that complacency is extremely risky.

In sum, there are times when our intuitions about what is safe are unreliable. A good carpenter does not equate to a good investment. When we buy a share, we cannot relax and assume that we know exactly what we have bought.

As Kenneth Arrow, a Nobel laureate in economics, wrote, "[Our] knowledge of the way things work, in society or in nature, comes trailing clouds of vagueness." We can never know exactly what will happen in the future. But, like the wanderer facing a sea of fog, we can try to blow away some of the clouds of vagueness so that we can better understand and manage risk.

Chapter 1

HOW TO
THINK ABOUT RISK

We have mentioned Paul Reichmann in our earlier comments. The Reichmanns are property moguls who bestrode the world until their huge empire collapsed in 1991. They provided rich material for one of the twentieth century's great business stories. Less well known is the fact that, in 1994, they very nearly pulled off a miraculous comeback. A few well-informed readers might recall that they entered a joint venture with George Soros, the famed speculator whose market-moving abilities have caused major controversies from Britain to Malaysia. But only a tiny number of people know that the Reichmanns disastrously blew a second chance to rescue themselves from oblivion, and they destroyed their venture with Soros in the bargain.

Having made and lost a fortune redeveloping vast swaths of cities such as New York, Toronto, and London, the humbled Reichmanns looked further afield in the early 1990s. In search of a new deal that would relaunch their operations, they hopped smartly onto a hot trend—the rise of new economies and so-called "emerging markets." Their dream was a multibillion-dollar development in the capital of one of the fastest-growing economies in the world. Mexico appeared poised on the brink of emergence into an established and accepted economic force. Its trade links with America and Canada were about to be ratified and liberalized via the North American Free Trade Agreement (NAFTA) treaty (signed by President Bill Clinton in 1993). But the city had very few modern office buildings, and rents were high in those that did exist. What could be more appropriate than to

revamp a chunk of the sprawling capital city and erect some of the Reichmanns' signature skyscrapers?

The Reichmann–Soros venture almost succeeded. The Reichmanns followed their typical development process. The venture
bought two parcels of land, one of which was on a prime site in the
heart of the city. The land was bought on favorable terms from the government, on the promise that it would be developed into a top-rate
site. By investing a relatively small amount in architects' drawings and
marketing, the Reichmanns hoped to lure a local partner into a 50:50
joint development venture. A giant publicity fanfare led to widespread
interest among big construction firms. ICA, a large local firm, bought
a 50 percent stake in the first parcel of land on the outskirts of the city.
In bidding for the second parcel, ICA proposed to be the builder as
well as a joint developer.

It seemed like a sure thing. ICA's cash would fund the entire development, leaving the Reichmanns and Soros with no downside exposure
but potentially tremendous upside prospects in the event that the project was a success. A further attraction for the Reichmanns was that they
had already dealt with ICA and felt that a deal could be closed quickly.

Unfortunately, the Reichmanns, like much of the rest of the world,
were overly convinced that Mexico's leaders, trained in American business schools, knew what they were doing. In 1994, the Mexican economy was under increasing pressure. Although inflation had fallen from
180 percent in 1987 to around 8 percent, growth was sluggish. The
Mexican currency was the victim of sudden bouts of nerves among
traders, which forced the government to intervene heavily in foreign exchange markets. The need to support the currency grew, and Mexico's
foreign exchange reserves dwindled from $25 billion in late 1993 to a
mere $6 billion a year later. But because the interventions had kept the
exchange rate fairly stable, few people watching the market had any idea
that big trouble was around the corner. If you were looking at the exchange rate to guide, say, an investment such as the Reichmanns', recent history would have given you little idea of what lay ahead.

The key to the peso's relationship to the dollar was a tight band within which the government insisted that it would stay. On December 20, 1994, the Mexican government announced that it had widened that band. The peso immediately fell by 10 percent, in a move that shocked traders and investors alike. On December 23, the band was removed altogether, and the peso went into free fall against the dollar, losing 50 percent of its value within just a few days. In addition, interest rates quadrupled over the same period. In the months that followed, it became clear that Mexico had suffered a major economic crisis.

How did the Reichmanns and George Soros react? Their deal with ICA was supposed to be signed and sealed on December 20. Mysteriously, in the days before that date, ICA began to stall. Perhaps it sensed that the currency was vulnerable. When the two sides met on December 21, ICA had changed its position. It wanted the 10 percent fall in the peso to be reflected in new terms for the deal. This was not entirely unreasonable; ICA had to use pesos to fund an investment that, in dollars, had suddenly become more expensive.

Ironically, the Reichmanns' partner might have thrown a lifeline, if only its right hand had known what its left hand was doing. George Soros's canny hedge fund traders had long since sold their peso holdings, believing the currency to be risky. But Soros's property arm had no such insight. It carried on as if everything was normal. No warning was sent to the Reichmann–Soros venture, which consequently had little sense of the ugly scenario that was about to unfold.

Assume the deal with ICA had been successfully renegotiated. What would have been the Reichmanns' position? Arguably, because the original deal had been a rich one, the new terms were simply slightly less rich. The Reichmanns still stood to make an extremely favorable deal with great upside. By signing a contract with ICA, they would have ensured that the project went ahead. They would then have recovered their sunk costs and been largely insulated from further falls in the peso. In effect, most of the future financial risk in the development would have been shouldered by ICA. The best scenario for the Reichmanns was a return of the peso to its former value, which could have added 10 percent to their upside. The worst scenario was that the peso would continue to fall and the deal could be lost altogether—a large downside.

Paul Reichmann, the family's most influential member, refused to deal. He would not allow any alteration to ICA's terms. Then things happened very fast. As the peso went into free fall after December 23, ICA saw that its timing for the development was lousy—the returns in dollars were insufficient to make the project worthwhile. Not surprisingly, it abruptly lost its appetite. The Reichmanns' comeback was off.

Imagine the scene in Mexico City on December 21. The Reichmanns had to ask themselves whether the initial peso devaluation would be the end of the matter, or whether there was more trouble to come. They might have done a simple analysis: What were financial markets telling them about the likelihood of further devaluations of the peso? A quick look at the currency options markets would have shown that traders indeed expected more bad news. Locking in terms at a 10 percent lower rate for the peso might turn out to be a bargain if it fell an additional 40 percent. However, a naive look at the past eighteen months of stable U.S./Mexican exchange rates would lull one into thinking that the current drop in rates was an aberration.

Instead, the Reichmanns chose a more subjective analysis, perhaps because they were committed to the idea of making a comeback. They concluded that the peso's troubles were temporary and that they should not make any concessions to ICA.

The point is that the Reichmanns bet everything on a single outcome. In effect, they were gambling that a single outlook for the peso would turn out to be correct. In fact, anything could have happened to the peso, so it really made sense to consider several possible outcomes. This is a key point about proper risk management that is often overlooked. When we plan around a single view of the future, we are actually gambling. Sensible planning requires us to consider a multitude of possible events and explore how each one might cause us to react.

Sources close to Paul Reichmann report that he carried on, trying to revive the deal and hoping that things could be ironed out. When it became clear that it would take many months to solve the problems in Mexico, Reichmann became more reclusive than ever and showed signs of rapid mood swings.* He was clearly suffering from serious Regret that he had so badly misjudged the situation.

Even though we may not always be conscious of it, we are all risk managers. As we navigate daily life, we must make a host of decisions that more or less explicitly reveal our attitude toward risk. Shall I travel by plane or train? Which detergent has fewer noxious chemicals? Which over-the-counter drug is less harmful? Should I buy a lottery ticket instead of a sandwich? Should I invest in mutual funds, stocks, or bonds? Which securities should I buy, and how long should I plan to own them? Should I give up smoking? Our views of risk are surprisingly idiosyncratic—one person's pleasure is another's poison. Hence the diversity of economic and business life.

There is a rich contemporary debate about the fine line between an acceptable and an unacceptable risk. From nuclear safety to food additives, we are bombarded with often contradictory and confusing information about risks. Is the tiny risk from using the chemical Alar on apples a price worth paying for its otherwise beneficial effects? If consumers had known more about ValuJet's safety record, would the airline have folded before the crash in the Everglades that killed so many persons? If the American money market funds that invested disastrously in complicated but supposedly yield-boosting derivatives in 1994 had been frank about the risks they were running in order to deliver slightly higher returns, would an investor boycott have forced the fund management firms to change the funds' approach before an expensive bailout became necessary? Would people have signed up to be "Names" at the Lloyd's insurance market in London if they had known how much

---

* As this book was going to press part of the deal with ICA was, in fact, successfully renegotiated.

downside risk was involved? Would so many banks have lent money
(which they subsequently lost in large amounts) to Robert Maxwell if
they had known more about the British tycoon's shaky finances? Why
did many of the same banks then take a further bath when they lent another fortune to the Eurotunnel, the project to build a tunnel under the
English Channel that was as successful in engineering terms as it was
hopeless in financial ones? The list of such questions is endless.

The list is also daunting, for these broad inquiries point to a central
confusion about risk management. At a societal level, we rely on governments to maintain or introduce regulations that are designed to
protect us from many excessive or unwarranted risks. The ban, in some
countries, on smoking in public is an obvious example, as are rules
about handling nuclear waste or processing uranium. Alternatively, institutions such as mutual societies and credit unions have arisen to extend access to risk management to large numbers of people. (Mutual
funds achieve the same purpose by virtue of their transactional efficiency.) In developed economies, these forms of "insurance" have
helped to spread financial security and well-being far more widely
than was previously the case.

But they have also helped to obscure a central and fundamental aspect of risk: each individual's attitude toward risk can often be at odds
with the attitudes of other people. In the blunt language of investing
and finance, how we feel about a particular risk depends greatly on our
unique circumstances, not the least of which is how rich or poor we
are, and whether (or when) we will need to get our hands on hard cash
as opposed to paper assets that represent real money in the future. Our
circumstances are unlikely to be precisely the same as everyone else's.
Even if two people end up making the same investment decision—for
example, to buy $1,000 worth of Citicorp stock—they will probably
have quite different reasons and motives for doing so. Further, there is
a common misperception that risk is purely an active concept, that it
only involves assuming danger in the hope of reward. In fact, risk

comes in other guises. If we have $1 million but choose to leave it under the mattress, then we are avoiding many risks. But we are just as certainly assuming others. There is risk in doing nothing, just as there is risk in taking action. Indeed, perhaps striking a balance between action and inaction is the essence of risk management.

From just this preliminary exploration, it should already be clear that risk is a remarkably subtle notion. Its meanings and boundaries shift constantly, making it difficult to pin down. An acceptable risk on one day might appear a foolish gamble on the next day. As we shall see, a way of thinking about risk that encompasses this subtlety has eluded generations of thinkers and researchers. Even in this age of high-tech computing, the basic architecture of risk management remains primitive. It is as if all that fancy technology is stored in the intellectual equivalent of a wooden shack.

Much has been written about risk in recent years. Indeed, an unprecedented amount of intellectual firepower has been directed at the subject, particularly in the field of finance. We only have to look at the recipients of Nobel prizes for economics during the past decade to see that great store is now set on the challenge of unmasking risk and explaining its finer points. Why does risk remain so elusive? One answer is that, for all of our sophistication, we sometimes shy away from asking simple questions, as if this avoidance makes it easier to grapple with difficult ones. Because great minds have battled with the meaning of risk, it seems presumptuous to suggest that we might need to start from first principles. Another answer is more humdrum. Rather than seek a comprehensive approach to risk, people have chosen "fit for purpose" solutions—the risk management equivalent of "quick and dirty" computer codes. For many business problems, that approach is sensible enough. But when investment and financial risks are involved, it borders on the cavalier. Why embrace an approach to risk that may be flawed, when the outcome could be disastrous? No professional gamblers would adopt such an approach; they know too much about ruin!

In *Against the Gods* (New York: John Wiley & Sons, 1996), Peter Bernstein describes how our understanding of risk and risk management has developed over the centuries. Until some central problems in mathematics and probability theory were solved, our ability to define and manage risk was necessarily limited. Moreover, developments in risk theory have been uneven. For generations, little would happen; then a burst of innovation and activity would bring thinking to a new plateau.

Bernstein asks rhetorically: What distinguishes thousands of years of history from what we think of as modern times? Human history has been chock full of brilliant individuals whose technological and mathematical achievements were astonishing; think of the early astronomers or the builders of the pyramids. The answer, suggests Bernstein, is our acceptance of risk: ". . . the notion that the future is more than a whim of the gods and that men and women are not passive before nature. Until human beings discovered a way across that boundary, the future was either a mirror of the past or the murky domain of oracles and soothsayers who held a monopoly over knowledge of anticipated events."

With helpful skepticism, Bernstein asks whether the fancy mathematics and computer wizardry of today are dangerously analogous to the graven images and idols before which earlier generations made their genuflections. If we rely too heavily on clever models and "black boxes," might we not be succumbing to an updated version of the faith that ancestors placed in deities and shamans? Indeed, might the false "science" of risk management be a dangerous illusion that itself hides potentially catastrophic risks?

Recent history tends to support this view. Until the dangers of risk management began to emerge during the 1980s, few ordinary people had heard of financial derivatives, for example—those infamous futures and options that supposedly caused a series of corporate blowups and disasters in the early 1990s. Few television-watching households have escaped at least a passing familiarity with derivatives. In Britain, for instance, the collapse in 1995 of Barings, an august and snobbish bank, led to the equivalent of a countrywide education program in modern finance.

Similarly, voters in Orange County, California, had an unexpected crash-course in finance in 1994, when their investment pool was so severely damaged that the county chose to declare itself bankrupt. How did this disaster happen? Robert Citron, the county's elected treasurer, had recklessly used "leverage," hoping to boost returns. In effect, this means taking on risks that are orders of magnitude larger than the underlying stake. He was found out by a big reversal in financial markets.

Some of the biggest and most respectable names in finance and business have fallen afoul of risk management in recent years. And there is no local or geographical monopoly on such disasters. Think of Britain's National Westminster Bank; Germany's Metallgesellschaft; America's Gibson Greetings, Merrill Lynch, and Bankers Trust; Japan's Daiwa Bank, Sumitomo, and IBJ— to name a few. Plenty of other firms have had problems, but they have chosen to cover them up rather than lose face and public confidence. Many banks, for example, have lost a few million dollars here and there as they have acquired trading and operating skills in the notoriously difficult options business.

One big bank was even the silent victim of an audacious robbery. Clever but criminal staff got inside an options pricing model and used tiny changes to skim off a few million dollars of profits for themselves. They were eventually caught, but the bank elected not to prosecute them. It feared (probably correctly, in light of other banks' experiences) that the revelation of the swindle could wipe out hundreds of millions of dollars of its overall value as nervous investors decided to place their money elsewhere.

It is impossible to calculate the real cost of risk management failures among businesses, but it certainly runs to many billions. In 1995 and 1996, documented losses were some $12 billion. Moreover, there are few signs that firms' reliance on mathematics and machines is diminishing. In the trading rooms that are the temples of modern finance, some of the world's brightest brains are competing to attain, however briefly, the strongest grip on risk. Therein lies competitive advantage—to put it crudely, the ability to wring huge profits from less-equipped rivals. These are the "model wars," a kind of intellectual and financial arms race that promises fat rewards to the victors.

Is there a danger of relying too much on models and not enough on common sense? We do not think there is too much reliance on models, for two main reasons. First, the past few decades have witnessed such rapid developments in finance theory and such growth in the world economy that the fact that many firms have occasionally fumbled is not surprising. The banks that have lost big money in options trades, for instance, have undoubtedly learned painful lessons. The best ones have adjusted their practices and grafted new rules and precautions onto older and sloppier systems so that they will not be similarly embarrassed in the future. For example, in 1987, Merrill Lynch, arguably the world's biggest investment bank, was embarrassed when it lost $377 million trading mortgage-backed securities. Since then, having installed new risk systems and maintained a careful watch over its trading, there has been no significant mishap.

Firms like Merrill Lynch probably have also absorbed the lesson that a risk might pop up somewhere else, quite unexpectedly. They can never relax; occasional losses, sometimes even big ones, are in the nature of life and business. That is why firms have money set aside as a cushion. It is known as equity, and it is there to fall back on in bad times. That is also why regulators require financial firms to set aside capital. Arguments about how much capital is the right amount are the main reason for the continued flourishing of risk management. Those who need the least capital to run the same risks can enjoy a profound competitive advantage. What we have seen to date in financial risk management at this level is perhaps best characterized as a series of related lessons about the dangers of innovation. But it is not a sign that there is some fatal flaw in modern efforts to improve our approach to risk. Indeed, it seems almost self-evident that if the costs of risk management really outweighed the massive benefits brought by a variety of new risk-sharing techniques, then the techniques would quickly have been rejected.

Our second reason for thinking that, in machines and mathematics, we have not reached a dangerous dead end is that thinking about risk has never been more widespread and has never been conducted at a higher level. The inadequacies of many existing approaches to risk have triggered a flourishing and fundamental debate, to which this book is a contribution.

Arguably, for the first time, risk is undergoing a comprehensive dissection, a process that simultaneously informs us in new detail and allows us to adopt and invent new techniques for risk sharing. Both in our ability to map and understand risk, and in our ability to build mechanisms that allow us to manipulate risk, far from being at a dead end, we are in an era of rich, astonishing, and (thanks to technology) possibly unprecedented progress.

Sharing the Risk

The idea of risk sharing is important but often neglected. As the voters in Orange County found out, a big loss, when spread among thousands or millions of people, causes only moderate or inconsequential pain for individuals. But where risks are concentrated, the results can be disastrous. Citibank nearly blew itself apart as recently as 1991 because it had made far too many loans to the real estate industry. It now carefully monitors its lending to avoid concentrations that could inflict similar damage. And it can use new financial instruments—credit derivatives, for example—that allow it to transfer to other banks, and to investors, risks that make it uncomfortable.

Consider an entrepreneur who has a 60 percent stake in her successful and fast-growing company but is overexposed to its fortunes and would be ruined if the firm failed. She would like to reduce that concentration by investing some of her paper wealth in other assets, and modern finance has come up with several ways to help her do just that. By giving up to other investors some of the upside potential of her stake, she can shelter her finances from an extreme negative outcome, such as her firm's going bust.

Risk sharing has a long history. Early financiers used the idea as the basis of today's insurance industry. Merchants and traders quickly learned that while they could be ruined individually by the loss of a single ship, they could quickly get rich if they joined together and formed fleets of ships that would not suffer unduly because of occasional wrecks. More than a century ago, mutually owned life insurance firms in America and Europe were able to extend the benefits of risk sharing to the masses, changing millions of people's lives.

A desire to manage risk and to profit from superior insight was just as prevalent among our ancestors as it is today. A random, simple, and intriguing example should suffice. In the fall of 1807, a group of middle-class women who lived in Arbois, a small town near Besançon, regional capital of the Jura, a rugged and little-known area of France that borders Alsace and Switzerland, undertook an amazing risk management transaction. The women ran a charitable concern, distributing food and material aid to poor people in the town and its surrounding villages. They laced their charity with a not-so-subtle dose of religion in the form of moral education. But theirs was a lay organization that functioned largely beyond the formal reach of the Catholic Church. The women displayed an acute sense of financial management in the conduct of their affairs. They sought out the best interest rates for any funds they collected, and they negotiated fiercely with local contractors to ensure that they were getting full value for their money when they purchased food.

In the course of their work, they traveled extensively in the town's environs. And they observed in 1807 that a rash of bad weather, following what had hitherto been a good growing season, had left much of that year's crop rotting in the fields. Instead of wringing their hands, they did something remarkable. They bought a futures contract that would lock in the price of grain that they would pay over the coming winter months. They paid 4 francs per measure for some 200 measures, rather than the 3 francs, 12 centimes that was the current market price. In that way, they knew that their charitable activities could continue in the harsh months when they contributed most in terms of welfare to the community. The fact that, had they been speculating, they would also have locked in a fat profit, probably did not occur to them. Today, the women can be imagined running their own investment club and, on the back of their successful trade, starring in their own public television investment show!

Better risk-sharing mechanisms could help many people to mute the effects of similar risks on their lives. For instance, if there were a market in housing derivatives (contracts that allowed us to bet on movements in house prices), someone worried about missing out on a big rise in prices could purchase options that would, in effect, pay out compensation to the nonowner. Similarly, owners could buy options that would give them downside protection in the event that the value of their house fell below the carrying cost of their mortgage.

Why don't such markets exist already? There are still plenty of practical barriers standing in their way. For instance, although the real estate market is far better understood these days, it remains relatively opaque, and prices are set rather arbitrarily. There is not yet sufficient reliable and regular price information to allow a meaningful derivatives market, particularly one that would be suitable for individuals. Also, there is no easily defined "standard house" that might be the basis for pro forma financial contracts. A home that one person thinks is a palace is an ugly pile to someone else. Similarly, before there could be a smoothly functioning market in "country risk," there would have to be a common definition of economic performance and some means of standardizing how each country measured its output.

It is likely, or perhaps inevitable, that such markets will be developed in the future, to satisfy the compelling power of risk sharing. Indeed, the idea of risk sharing—insurance—is central to our new framework for risk. We are not suggesting that insurance is the same thing as risk, or that, of itself, insurance is all that is needed for effective risk management. Our framework is more flexible than that. Rather, we want to suggest that if a risk can be understood, then, using modern financial techniques, it should be possible to devise ways of hedging/distributing that risk. And once that can be done, risks can be managed in two directions. Some people will be keen to take on more risk, and others will be glad to pay a premium to shed some or all of it. These responses to risk form the basis of a market in which a natural competition between buyers and sellers creates real and transparent prices. Where plenty of risks are traded with transparent prices, it is even possible for individuals and firms to "optimize" their risk exposures—that is, they can select those exposures that, for an equivalent level of risk, are likely to produce the highest returns, and they can sell their less efficient assets.

This is not pie in the sky or wishful thinking. In June 1997, for instance, a novel transaction launched in America attracted huge interest from investors around the world. Ask most investors if they would like to share the hurricane damage risk of a big insurer and they would probably balk—all that talk of "El Niño" might have been a tad unnerving. But consider the following bet that was offered by a leading insurer: you buy a one-year security that yields 11 percent (well above yields on bonds that carry similar credit ratings); in return, you buy into an 80 percent share of the risk that a single hurricane season will cause the insurer losses of more than $1 billion but only up to $1.5 billion. In other words, if the worst happens during a single hurricane season, you will lose all of your principal. Once the insurer has lost more than $1 billion, you will be on the hook for your share of the $400 million maximum exposure. Would you take this bet?

On the face of it, the answer is unclear. So before you decide, you might ask a few questions. How much have past hurricanes cost the insurer—in this case, United Services Automobile Association (USAA), a firm that specializes in insuring members and veterans of America's military and their families? Hurricane Andrew, the worst storm to hit Florida and the southern coastal states in recent history, cost USAA $555 million of losses in 1992. Fine; but how much would, say, the horrendous storm of 1926 cost USAA if it happened again today? Using a computer simulation to model that storm's impact, the answer is $800 million. There would be no loss on your stake. So the bet is beginning to look reasonably attractive. Indeed, do some fancier computer modeling to generate possible storms that could occur in the future, and let the virtual weather rage for 10,000 years, and you find that the likelihood of USAA's experiencing a loss greater than $1 billion is less than 1 percent. The chance of a loss of more than $1.5 billion is less than four-tenths of 1 percent. By now, you might be reaching for your checkbook.

That is just what some sixty institutional investors, including banks and mutual funds, did. From mid-June 1997 until the end of that year's hurricane season, they were avid watchers of the Weather Channel; for as long as the hurricane season lasted, they were exposed to a unique form of risk. Were USAA required to pay damages, some $313 million of investors' money was at risk; an additional $164 million was tied up in a second set of securities that carried a lower return but guaranteed the principal amount for less-risk-seeking folk. For a deal that started out trying to raise $150 million, that represented a huge success.

One reason for its success was that the attraction of the securities for investors went far beyond the probabilities of the single bet they were offered. Until such deals began to appear—the first widely syndicated offering was launched in December 1996 for a broad portfolio of risks underwritten by St. Paul Re, subsidiary of a big insurer based in Minnesota—investors could only gain exposure to the reinsurance (that is, the insurance of the existing insurance risk) market by buying the shares of reinsurers. However, that is an inefficient and unreliable way of capturing reinsurance risk.

Because they are uncorrelated to the returns from financial markets, the returns from pure reinsurance risks such as those offered in the USAA deal are highly desirable for investors who are otherwise limited to financial assets. When share and bond prices might be tumbling, chances are that reinsurance returns will hold up fine. Adding reinsurance risk to a portfolio should therefore significantly lower its overall volatility—which, after all, is one of the basic tenets of modern portfolio theory.

For this important reason, investment bankers have high hopes for the nascent market in so-called catastrophe insurance bonds, and the rest of us should take note. The technique expands the overall ability of insurers and reinsurers to spread risk around. At present, they play a sophisticated game of "passing the parcel" among professionals. But if they can offer pure insurance risks to investors, they can tap vast new demand while avoiding the unnecessary expense of buying cover from their competitors. In time, that should make insurance cheaper (because less volatile) and hence more ubiquitous. Insurance risk will, in effect, become a new asset class alongside shares, bonds, and commodities.

Another impact of catastrophe reinsurance has perhaps the greatest potential to change financial markets. At present, large industrial firms have a constant insurance dilemma. It would be too costly to insure every bus, truck, and piece of equipment they own. Consequently, many companies choose to "self-insure." An oil refiner, for example, will assume all of the risk that one of its plants might be destroyed by a disastrous fire, betting that, over time, the returns from its other assets will cover the loss more cheaply than if it were to buy continuous cover. Insurance bonds can change that. A refiner might choose instead to package some of its business risk and offer it, in the form of securities, to investors. It would, in effect, strip away that risk from its underlying operations, which would, in turn, affect the risk profile of its other issued securities. (By implication, the price of its shares should rise.) In essence, the financial technology that creates reinsurance bonds can be used to develop a class of risk that was previously undiversifiable. Provided the risks are carefully defined and can be priced to attract investors, there should be no lack of demand for such bonds.

Anyone who can understand these related ideas is well on the way to grasping the essences of modern finance, even if the arcane language of derivatives and portfolio theory still seems foreign. In the chapters that follow, we will explore these ideas in more detail. But our next step moves backward. Before we explain a new framework for managing risk, we need to lay out the basic building blocks of risk and risk management—the pieces that we need if we are to understand and control risk.

Chapter 2

THE ELEMENTS OF
RISK MANAGEMENT

A few simple ideas about risk and how we can manage it are sufficient to unlock many otherwise impenetrable questions. For instance, at the most basic level, why are we motivated even to define and to manage risk? The answer is that we worry about what might happen in the future. We know that we are likely to have an array of experiences—some pleasurable, some painful, some potentially fatal. At the very least, we are strongly motivated to avoid or minimize our exposure to the latter. For investors, this means avoiding relative as well as outright losses.

Very little of existing risk management embraces the basic idea that when we think about risk, we are, by definition, looking forward in time. As we saw in the brief history of risk in Chapter 1, there has been a strong tendency to evaluate risk by looking at what has happened in the past. That idea—the extrapolation of the past into the future—is not entirely stupid if it is used with care. Very often, however, large institutions and individuals alike adopt this flawed concept (or variations of it) as the main basis for their management of risk. And that approach, whether from the viewpoint of managers whose jobs depend on success, or of shareholders whose money is at stake, is decidedly scary.

Only a few central elements are required to create a risk management architecture that is as robust as it is flexible. Our starting point is a definition of risk:

Risk is a measure of the potential changes in value that will be experienced in a portfolio as a result of differences in the environment between now and some future point in time.

This definition clearly covers financial risk—the possibility that we might own a share that falls in value over the coming year. But by capturing the notion of a *portfolio*, we think we have also covered more general forms of risk. As we will see, each of us owns a portfolio whether or not we think of it as such. Thus, our risks include things such as whether we crash our car or win the lottery, as well as things more obviously related to changes in the prices of financial assets such as mutual funds.

With this definition in mind, we now explore the main elements required for forward-looking risk management.

- Time Horizon: Over what period of time are we concerned to consider our exposure to risk?
- Scenarios: What events could unfold in the future and how would they affect the value of our investments?
- Risk Measure: What is the unit we are using to gauge our exposure to risk?
- Benchmarks: What are the points of comparison against which we can measure our performance?

Let's examine these elements one by one.

Time Horizon

The first thing we need to know is our time horizon. Over what period of time are we hoping to manage risk? If we think just about the risk of investing money and losing some of it, for instance, someone retiring next week will have a very different time horizon from someone who just started a first job. A soon-to-be pensioner might recoil in horror from an investment that has a big risk of losing money in return for a big payoff, but will be over in a few days. The potential gain is not worth the risk of losing money that soon will be needed to provide a regular monthly income. By contrast, a new worker might readily embrace the same investment, thinking that a loss in the next few days can be overcome by superior returns in the years that will follow.

This was clearly demonstrated on October 27, 1997, when the New York Stock Exchange suffered its biggest-ever one-day fall. Commentators on that evening's news broadcasts almost unanimously pointed out that the only people who should really worry about the collapse were those very close to retirement. All other investors were told to remind themselves that they were in stocks for the long haul! Our personal time horizons should change in line with our circumstances. A new worker might alter his or her time horizon to reflect life events. Marriage and children, with their associated costs, can entirely shift the length of time over which a person wishes to view the future.

Even this simple idea hides complexities. Most people will adopt more than one time horizon in the course of their lives, but they may also have multiple horizons at a given moment. They might have some assets to which they attribute a very long horizon—a young worker's retirement fund, for instance. (In the extreme case, some young workers might choose not to have a retirement fund—their time horizon simply does not stretch that far.) Other assets will be treated with much greater immediacy. By implication, time horizons help to determine how we feel about different aspects of our overall exposure.

We can easily make mistakes if we fail to think carefully about the time element of risk. Imagine that we take on a substantial mortgage in order to buy a big fixer-upper house. We stretch our finances as far as we can because we love the long-term potential of the renovated property. But then interest rates rise by 2 percent, pushing up the cost of our mortgage. Suddenly our time horizon has shrunk dramatically. We no longer think about choosing paint colors for the long term. Instead, we worry about how to survive financially today. The idea that we can afford to renovate the house has simply retreated until better times return.

In the 1920s and 1940s, economists such as Frank Knight and George Shackle learned to distinguish between risk (what can be quantified with certainty) and uncertainty (the inability to know for sure what will happen in the future). When we choose a time horizon, we are implicitly choosing a period over which we wish to describe the uncertainty of what lies ahead.

Scenarios

Our second requirement for risk management is to develop scenarios that describe what could happen in the future. In essence, a scenario is a series of linked observations about the state of the world at some predetermined future time. To understand the concept better, let's look at how George Shackle grandly and brilliantly described a decision:

> Decision . . . is the imagining of rival paths of affairs; the assigning of these paths to the respective actions, amongst those the decision maker can envisage, which seem to make them possible; and the resolving upon that action which, at best, offers a sequel more powerfully out-weighing what it threatens at worse, than any rival action.

In other words, whether consciously or intuitively, we use scenarios ("rival paths") when we make decisions and when we imagine what might happen—good and bad— in the future. We include in them everything we think is relevant to us, or at least everything that seems to be relevant. There is always a scenario that includes something we had not thought of!

Scenarios are part of everyday life. Politicians deal in scenarios as a stock in trade. Think of the phrase "a heartbeat away from the presidency." It verbalizes a future scenario in which a vice president steps into the top job because a country's leader has just died. Media and academic pundits who monitor pre-election trends also make a living by spinning scenarios: What if the conservatives win 250 seats? And so on. A good example is Canada's ongoing debate over the constitutional status of Quebec. In the scenario of that province's future independence, investors based outside Canada face a novel proposition and will likely revise their attitude toward the riskiness of Canada. Banks in Canada are known to hedge (in effect, to protect themselves by buying insurance) against extreme interest rate moves each time the constitutional question is revisited. Similarly, debate in Britain about constitutional reforms such as devolution of Scotland and Wales requires speculation about how power might be divided in the future. What will happen to the Labour government's huge majority under different scenarios, and what will happen to Britain's tax system if large parts of the country become semiautonomous? Equally, what are the implications, under different policies, of Britain's putative membership in the European Monetary Union?

Another big user of scenarios is the military. It has become a staple of conflict planning to model the different scenarios that might determine, say, a combined land–sea attack. What if the weather is cloudy? Could there be a sandstorm that will reduce the mobility of ground units? What would happen to projected casualty rates if the enemy has 10 percent more troops than reported by surveillance? Such questions were commonplace in the Gulf War in 1991. Military commanders these days also use scenarios in sophisticated computer models and programs to play war games that simulate live combat situations. These are much more than fancy video games. Indeed, such techniques are instructive to watch in action. At a high-tech research laboratory in Malibu, California, field officers model combat using a simulator that sets a scenario and then plays out battles. Commanders can assess the field and then deploy their troops as they see fit. The modelers learn from the outcomes how the best soldiers make effective choices. By building such "captured knowledge" into regular training for all officers, the performance of real soldiers should improve, resulting in

fewer casualties. Similarly, many pilots these days are trained "virtually"—they rarely fly a real airplane, learning instead on sophisticated
flight simulators that can be programmed with different scenarios.

Scenarios give us a basis for evaluating how we might feel about different possible outcomes in the future, which in turn will shape how
we will make decisions. This is another area where our individual feelings play a role. As investors, for instance, we all face the same sets of
possible outcomes. But our willingness to accept some outcomes and
reject others varies, as do our time horizons. Individually, we will probably attach quite different weights to the variables that we use when we
model our scenarios.

How we feel about a scenario will depend on whether we think it is
likely to occur. In the real world, if we were to embrace a single scenario, we would be putting all our eggs in one basket. Instead of managing risk, we would be counting on a single outcome. In effect, we
would be forecasting as if we knew with certainty what was about to
happen. Entire businesses have been brought to their knees by "single-
scenario forecasting." Nor have individuals been infallible. Think of
those people who assumed that the value of houses or the price of mutual funds would always rise. They should have put greater weight on
scenarios in which fund prices fell, or rising interest rates made coping
with a big mortgage far more difficult.

If we are to understand and use scenarios properly, we will generally
need lots of them to take into account a wide range of possibilities.
And we will need to take into account the possibility that something
disastrous might lie in the future. Even if we accord them only a very
small weight, reflecting the fact that they are extremely unlikely to
occur, our very acknowledgment of nasty scenarios will alert us to otherwise hidden risks.

Scenarios, then, are powerful tools for reducing the uncertainty we
face when we look forward. Some scenarios, particularly short-term
ones, can reasonably be based on historical precedents. If a share is
priced at $10, typically moves by around 50 cents, and has never

moved by more than $2 up or down in a single trading day, it might be reasonable to choose a one-day scenario in which the price is essentially stable. Other scenarios, however, are useful precisely because they include the possibility of a sudden change that overturns all our assumptions. As we will see later, it is vital for good risk management that we consider scenarios that make us uncomfortable, even if we feel certain that nasty outcomes will not occur. What if the one day we care about turns out to be the day when our share price tumbles to $4 because the firm announced terrible earnings?

Scenarios do not solve everything, but they represent a big improvement on the "forecasting" that is so prevalent in business and ordinary life. If we were asked to forecast the value of a bond portfolio in one year's time, we would have to admit defeat—we simply do not know the answer. But it is relatively easy to come up with a set of scenarios that captures likely and extreme values for the portfolio.

Without scenarios on the future, it is impossible to develop a coherent framework for risk management. The force of this point can be neatly demonstrated by a series of questions. Assume for a moment that we are running a company that has a portfolio of businesses. (It could just as well be an investment portfolio containing a combination of assets.) What do we think will happen in the future? We have selected our portfolio because we think it stands a good chance of generating returns that we can use to pay staff and leave a profit on the table (see Figure 2.1). But is it possible that our judgment is wrong? Might we have made a poor selection of businesses that will go horribly wrong and force us into bankruptcy? That is certainly possible, even though we think it unlikely. By implication, we agree that there is more than one possible outcome in the future. We could do fine or do badly.

Logically, if there are two possible outcomes, then there must be a third: perhaps we will achieve only average results, just well enough to break even. By now, even the most hardened skeptic should see that the number of future outcomes is infinite. If we focus on only a single outcome, we are making a big mistake because so many other things might

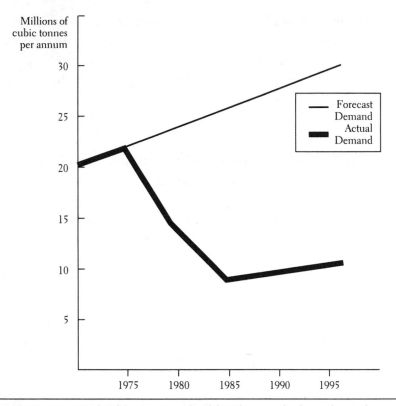

FIGURE 2.1 To build or not to build? This graph shows how planners usually make a forecast. The broad line shows the actual shipping tonnage required in the period from 1975 to 1995. The narrow line shows what an industry forecaster predicted would be required in the same period based on demand in the preceding period. Single-scenario planning of this kind is dangerous: such forecasts rarely match actual outcomes.

happen. We cannot adequately manage our risks unless we examine them across a wide range of scenarios. We cannot review all possible scenarios—that task is futile for risk management because it would take more time and computing power than we have available. Rather, we should concentrate our firepower on those scenarios that we should care most about avoiding.

Scenarios and Strategic Planning

It is shocking to realize the prevalence of such forecasting. Kees van der Heijden, a professor at Strathclyde University in Britain, has described the role scenarios can play in a firm's strategic planning. Based on his years at Royal Dutch/Shell, an international oil group that has been a pioneer of scenario planning, he shows how fallible businesses can be unless they accept the limits of forecasting.

Every four years, over a twenty-year period, the Association of West European Shipbuilders published forecasts of the worldwide demand for shipbuilding (see Figure 2.2). The forecasts were consistently in error because planners assumed that the recent trends would continue. For someone running a shipyard, these supposedly helpful forecasts were actually worse than useless. They were positively dangerous, because they gave the impression of certainty where none existed.

Van der Heijden has also examined the impact of the 1973 oil crisis. Since the end of the Second World War, oil companies had been used to steady growth in demand. There was little focus on strategic planning because 6 or 7 percent annual growth was seen as reliable. Oil firms simply added new capacity and assumed that growing demand would make it economic. When the oil crisis hit (see Figure 2.3), firms continued to pile on capacity as if nothing had happened. It took the industry two years before the growth in capacity slowed down, and another five or six years before the industry significantly altered its behavior. That lag can be measured in billions of dollars of wasted construction and price pressure caused by overcapacity.

There was a similar delay before oil firms began ordering fewer tankers. Once they woke up, there was a dramatic drop in demand for tankers while the overcapacity that had built up worked its way through the system. Many readers might remember pictures from the late 1970s of hundreds of idle and empty tankers stranded in anchorages around the world, while many in the shipping industry will

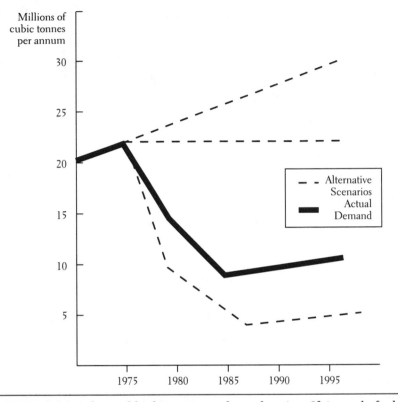

FIGURE 2.2   A forward-looking approach to planning. If, instead of relying on a single-scenario forecast, shipping industry planners had considered a variety of scenarios, they would have been in a much better position to deal with adverse outcomes. This graph shows how alternate forecasts of demand bracket actual demand. A key to constructing scenarios is to consider extremes in either direction.

recall the disastrous effect the overcapacity had on freight shipping rates.

Van der Heijden then asks: What if, by using scenarios, a firm had been able to adjust its business to suit conditions in the space of a single year rather than three or four? Think of the ensuing competitive

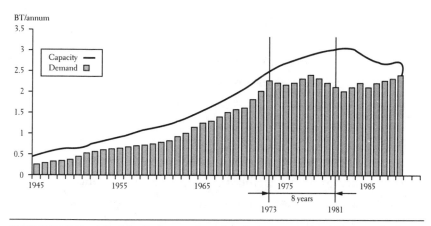

FIGURE 2.3 World oil demand and refining capacity. This graph shows how oil industry capacity, represented by the black line, continued to rise even as demand (represented by vertical bars) for oil fell following the 1973 oil crisis and, again, later in the 1970s and 1980s. Firms were slow to react to altered circumstances.

advantage. Suppose more firms had been prepared to think the unthinkable? Imagine sitting in a strategy meeting at IBM in 1980. The group is discussing the future market for the Personal Computer (PC). The market forecast says there will be 275,000 PCs in use in a decade's time, so it seems obvious that IBM should outsource the machine's operating system and chips. Now, suggests van der Heijden, suppose an outsider walks into the room and announces that the market will in fact be 60 million and counsels against giving business away to rivals such as Microsoft and Intel. That person would probably have been laughed at, but the example illustrates the potential of scenarios to change how we think. If anyone had considered the economic impact such a scenario might have had on IBM, the more likely recommendation to the firm would have been: Hedge your bets. For instance, a tougher contract with Microsoft would have brought cheap protection from a "fallout" scenario.

Risk Measures

The next thing we need for risk management is a risk measure: What unit will we use to gauge the riskiness of what we are proposing to do? This observation seems so basic. Surprisingly, however, measurement of risk is one of the biggest challenges in finance.

We have already observed that traditional risk management has tended to impose broad measures on everyone, rather than (correctly) tailoring measures to specific risk appetites. It is widely accepted, among financial managers and people who run businesses, that broad risk measures can have limited application and even dangerous characteristics. A simple example comes from a technique known as Value at Risk (VaR). This measure is used to describe how much money ("value") is at risk in a firm or bank at a given moment in a given period. Although it appears to reduce risk to an easy-to-understand number, it can disguise or overlook terrifying risks by virtue of its simplifications. It offers managers little guidance as to where risks are lurking in their organization. For example, two trading desks might generate exactly the same VaR number, even though the Russian bond-trading desk is clearly riskier than the French equities desk.

In addition, there has been a widespread tendency to separate how we measure risk from how we make investment decisions. In other words, we have suffered from a disconnect between the units we use to account for risk and the metric we apply when we allocate our economic and financial resources. In a comprehensive risk framework, these should be closely related.

Benchmarks

Risk measurement is linked to another poorly understood area of risk management—our need for a benchmark, something we can use when we must make comparisons between different things. Without a point of comparison, we have no idea how one experience has turned out relative to another.

Benchmarks are like scenarios in that we are always using them, even if unconsciously. When we buy something, we usually look at alternatives and ask ourselves whether we are getting the best deal. Someone may have told us about the bargain they got on something and that price becomes our benchmark when we go shopping for the same item ourselves. We are always making comparisons that involve a benchmark. If we are dissatisfied because our friends are all living in bigger houses than we can afford, and are driving fancier cars, that is because we feel we are underperforming the benchmark of material comfort by which we are measuring our success. If four colleagues earn promotions while we are continually passed over, we feel that we are underperforming the benchmark of corporate success. In both cases, we have to ask whether these benchmarks are right for us. We might live in a smallish house and drive an old wreck, but if we drink fine wines every day and take expensive vacations, then we should adopt a more appropriate benchmark.

The idea of benchmarks has not escaped modern finance. Indeed, the industry is littered with benchmarks designed to describe how markets and groups of instruments have performed. Think of the intense competition between, say, the Dow Jones Industrial Average and the Standard & Poor's 500, not to mention the Russell 2000 index, to be the best measure of the health of the American stock market. But an important aspect of a helpful benchmark has been largely overlooked. Remember the observation that we all have our own attitude toward risk? We should therefore all have our own benchmark, one that is appropriate to our view of the world. A proper benchmark should be designed to reflect the context of its user and the context in which it is being used. Further, we need to grasp that a benchmark is not a static thing. Just as the results of what we actually do will depend on the scenarios that unfold, so our benchmark, if it has been properly chosen, will be affected by the same factors that define those scenarios. In other words, and counterintuitively, a benchmark is a fluid concept. At different times and reflecting changing circumstances, we might choose one benchmark in favor of another.

Risk-Adjusted Valuation

These four elements—time horizon, scenarios, risk measure, and benchmarks—are the essential building blocks of forward-looking risk management. With these elements in place, we can begin to do some remarkable things. Once we have a sound basis for comparing the relative riskiness of things, we can accurately measure risk-adjusted valuation. If we know how much risk we have taken for a given level of performance, then we can determine whether we have been adequately rewarded. To put it another way, we can give true expression to our appetite for risk. Risk-adjusted valuation gives us a tool to help us decide one path or another when we look ahead at an uncertain future.

A helpful way to understand this concept is to think of it in terms of self-insurance. When we face a risky deal, we can choose whether to insure ourselves. Typically—because, as Peter Bernstein put it, we are "against the gods"—we need insurance—the chances are that sometimes we will lose, and we will need a cushion to catch us. If we do not buy insurance, then we are self-insuring; implicitly, we are indicating that we have sufficient money to cover the loss. If we choose to insure, then we will often adopt an element of self-insurance by choosing a deductible. To reach a risk-adjusted valuation, we should price into deals the cost of insurance, regardless of whether we self-insure or buy protection. In other words, proper valuation acknowledges the cost of our potential losses. Imagine that we want to buy a $20,000 diamond ring. If we were to lose the ring, the replacement cost might well be beyond our means. We cannot afford to self-insure, so we need to factor into our purchase the annual premium for the insurance that will protect us against loss. We then have a risk-adjusted price for the ring. We may be forced to decide that we cannot afford the ring, even though we have saved the $20,000 ticket price. By contrast, if we buy a $100 child's bicycle, we might happily self-insure. The replacement cost is small, so the deal remains affordable even after that amount is reflected in the price. We can reach a risk-adjusted valuation if we think of it as a form of mental accounting for the replacement cost, in the event of loss.

Risk-adjusted measures are extremely powerful tools. They have the potential to change the way millions of people behave and the choices they make. In essence, one should never make a decision or take an action based on absolute prices or returns. Indeed, a principal purpose of this book is to encourage people to think in terms of risk-adjusted measures.

Finally, we need a measure that allows us to compare the risk/reward characteristics of two alternative outcomes. Only with such a measure can investors make informed trade-offs when they choose, say, between two mutual funds. Such a measure is entirely lacking from most investment choices today. We suggest how a measure might be formulated and then applied to help people balance their fear of losing money and their desire to make it. This approach allows them to produce a range of exposures that has the greatest risk-taking efficiency. In effect, they can optimize their risk taking.

This risk architecture is rich in complexity and subtlety. Before we explain how it works in practice, however, we need to introduce some ways of visualizing risk.

Visualizing Risk

In different ways and to different degrees, all of us are constantly exposed to possible outcomes, good and bad. The simplest way to see our overall exposure is as an array of positions on a two-dimensional

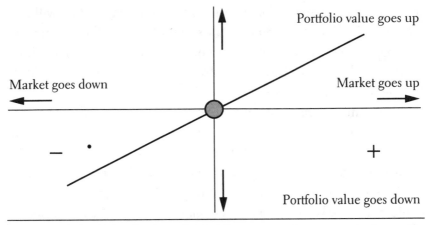

FIGURE 2.4 A simple view of risk. The center point represents the portfolio we hold today. The black line represents our exposure to future changes in value. These could be either up or down.

chart (Figure 2.4). The "thing" represented could be something as complex as our entire finances or as relatively simple as a small portfolio of investments. In the latter case, the portfolio has the potential either to rise or fall in value, but it is made up of a mixture of smaller positions, some of which might indeed rise while others fall. The two-dimensional snapshot view shows this mix of upside and downside potential outcomes. When we own a portfolio we are exposed to all of those outcomes; our net gain or loss will be the sum of the outcomes. In the language of finance, we have a "long" position in the portfolio.

Variables

A richer view of risk is provided by the more complex chart in Figure 2.5. Imagine that we take our simple view and lay it out somewhat differently. Change in the value of our portfolio at the present moment is represented by one axis. On either side of it are negative and positive

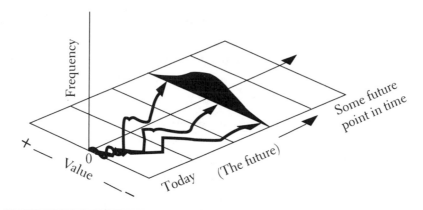

FIGURE 2.5   Risk in future. Viewed from today (the point indicated by 0 on the graph), our portfolio may be worth either more or less than its current value. The likelihood of a particular value being achieved is indicated by the curve—whether it is weighted more to the positive or negative side of the central axis.

values; we know that we could make or lose money going forward. As we project into the future, the value of our portfolio will be affected by many different market variables: interest rates, exchange rates, growth rates, yields, and so on. The jagged lines represent possible future impacts on our portfolio of these variables.

The process of identifying and mapping these risk variables is a key part of risk management. Unfortunately, it is also difficult. Remember that we are creating a model of the world by abstracting from reality. The world is extremely complex, and we cannot hope to model it in all its diversity and unexpectedness. Even for a simple portfolio there might be dozens of risk variables. For a complicated portfolio, or for a simulation of a family's overall exposures, there could be a million variables. Mathematically, coping with even a dozen variables requires great skill and computational muscle because, to do the job properly, we have to know (1) how each variable affects the others and (2) how to take those effects into account for the overall result. The trick in risk management is to identify the most important variables—the ten or so that will account for 90 percent of the end result—and to exclude as many of the meaningless elements of the variable set as we can confidently identify. An American investor, for instance, might choose to exclude Bulgarian interest rates (although a Bulgarian investor might not feel the same way about U.S. rates). Similarly, an investor who only invests in assets denominated in his or her home currency might ignore exchange rates. (This constrained approach to investing might not produce the best risk-adjusted returns.)

There are many potential values, depending on what happens. For risk management purposes, we need to know what constitutes a good selection of those potential values. That is where our time horizon comes in. Let's say that each line on the grid in Figure 2.5 represents three months. Our time horizon is then nine months. Using scenarios that alter the balance of the variables we have chosen, and weighting each scenario to reflect how likely we think it is, we can calculate the different outcomes for our portfolio. Each set of scenarios will produce a different result; in this case, we have shown how three outcomes will produce more (or less) return in the future. Figure 2.6 shows a different way of viewing the future using these scenarios, but one which makes explicit that outcomes can be negative as well as positive. If we calculate lots of results, then we can begin to array them from best to worst. That ranking, in effect, produces a line showing how our future outcomes are distributed and how that distribution is weighted. If the line "bulges" in one direction, then there are more positive outcomes than negative ones, and vice versa. In the example in Figure 2.5, the distribution is quite even and close to what mathematicians and statisticians refer to as a "bell-shaped curve." But remember how we have stressed always including scenarios that will produce some negative outcomes? Any curve that bulged only to the left of today's value might look like an attractive bet, close to a sure thing, when, in fact, it might be an extremely risky bet because the scenarios have been skewed toward the positive.

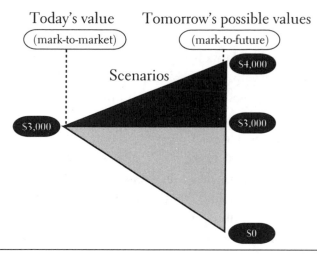

Today's value Tomorrow's possible values

(mark-to-market) (mark-to-future)

Scenarios

$4,000

$3,000 $3,000

$0

FIGURE 2.6 Marking-to future. In this example, the value of your portfolio today is $3,000. If you choose to enter into this deal, there is a chance that it may increase in value to $4,000 over the given period. There is also a chance that it will decrease to $0. Therefore, your decision has an Upside of $1,000 and a possible Regret of $3,000.

We have constructed quite a complex and multidimensional picture of risk. It is forward-looking, so it helps us to keep in mind the most important risk management questions. It uses scenarios that incorporate the key risk variables that will affect our future over a specified time horizon. And it neatly shows us how our portfolio will react under different scenarios.

This is the essential idea behind the "Marking-to-Future"* method that was developed by Ron Dembo for the practical measurement of banks' risk. As represented in Figure 2.6, the method suggests why we

---

*"Marking to future" is a new concept developed by one of the authors. For a more detailed explanation, see Ron S. Dembo, "Marking to Future," in Carol Alexander (Ed.), *A Handbook of Risk Management* (New York: John Wiley, 1998).

think that our risk elements combine to form a new paradigm for measuring risk. By adding the concept of a benchmark, the diagram reminds us that risk decisions always have to be grounded in an ability to compare the outcomes with measurable analogues. Note that in the scenarios box we have smoothed out the performance lines of our earlier three-scenario portfolio model. Each line forms the "branch" of a simple "tree" connecting today's value with possible values tomorrow. Each branch may be accorded a weight or probability that reflects how likely we think it is to occur in relation to the other branches. (Even in a very complicated tree, the sum of those probabilities must equal 100 percent.) Trees will be featured in some later chapters of this book, so it is important that we understand what they represent. Chapter 3 explains how they can help us to advance our thinking about risk.

Chapter 3

OF DECISIONS AND RISK

Financial risk is measured in a number of ways. Many of these measures are based on probability, typically expressed as: "There is an 80 percent chance that you will earn a 7 percent return, but a 20 percent chance that you will lose one-third of your investment." Yet most of our decisions are for one time only; we face them on a single occasion. For these one-time decisions, the probability of an outcome is not necessarily appropriate because probability measures the average over a very long run of the same bet. If we buy a lottery ticket, we will naturally want to know the probability of winning. But chances are we won't analyze the lottery on this basis. We won't have the luxury of being able to play the lottery over and over again until our final result approximates what the probability measure is telling us.

What we need, then, is a way to analyze one-time situations. Peter Bernstein himself has embraced this position. In a lecture given in 1997, he addressed the issue of "How do we decide?" He noted that there is a persistent tension between the probabilities that are based on measurement and the probabilities that come from our gut: "[W]hat do we do when the probability of one outcome is much greater than the probability of another outcome, but the consequences of being wrong are much greater for the outcome with the lower probability?" In the end, those consequences must dominate the probabilities.

Economists have long known that we mainly tend to face one-time decisions, yet much formal economics assumes the opposite. This contradiction has led to some memorable outbursts. In 1958, for instance, George Shackle made a trenchant case:

> To most businesses it falls only once or twice, or a handful of times, to have to decide upon the purpose, type, scale and location of an individual plant; most professional men choose a career only once; and so on. These occasions of choosing are spread at such long and irregular intervals that they cannot be treated as together forming a seriable experiment. . . . What is the sense of a weighted average that adds together a hundred falsehoods and one truth after multiplying each by some irrelevant number?

This represents perhaps the strongest objection to probability-based decision making.

How we think about the choices that we face can usually be couched in terms of risk. What is the risk of doing A versus B or C? The answer is clearly relative. How will we feel if we choose one course over another, particularly if it turns out after the event that we have made a bad choice? How do we relate our knowledge of each option's absolute risk to our own circumstances and consequent tolerance for relative risk?

The answers to these questions are difficult, partly because our intellectual understanding of risk is surprisingly less advanced than our intuitive sense of it. Because of its complex nature, it is difficult for us to model risk in ways that are useful in the real world. Indeed, our typical mathematical descriptions of risk (for which Nobel prizes have been awarded) can prove dangerous if they are applied scrupulously in the real world.

This is best illustrated by the following simple example. In your hand you have $10. You must decide which of two mutual funds to invest your money in for one month. Because each fund holds different assets, there will be a different set of outcomes in the event that market circumstances change in particular ways during the month.

For example, depending on whether interest rates stay the same, or move up or down, there will be different effects on the funds. If assigned a probability, each possible event will have an effect on the investment outcome that you know in advance. This is where our tree picture of risk comes in handy.

Figure 3.1 shows the Mark-to-Future diagram for Fund A. To understand how complicated the notion of risk is, think of the different ways one might analyze the risks of this proposed investment.

There is a 20 percent (that is, one in five) chance that you will lose money, but an 80 percent (four in five) chance that you will gain something.

You can be 90 percent confident under the possible scenarios that you will lose no more than $6 of your original $10. Indeed, there is an 80 percent certainty that you will lose no more than $2.

This approach focuses on how much of your present value you have *at risk*—hence, it is known as Value-at-Risk (VaR). This measure of

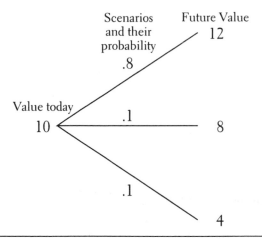

FIGURE 3.1   Mark-to-future for Fund A. The initial stake, $10, is to be invested for one month. Thanks to possible events, such as movements in interest rates, there is an 80 percent chance that the stake will rise to $12, a 10 percent chance that it will fall to $8, and a 10 percent chance that it will fall to $4.

risk has become a standard by which banks and other financial firms try to measure their exposure to potential losses. It has even been sanctioned by international regulators as a sensible way for firms to measure risk. (See Chapter 5 for a longer discussion of VaR.)

In Fund A, you know that your absolute VaR is $6.

Another approach to risk takes into account the fact that, over time, there is some average outcome arising from the three possibilities. Look again at your three possible outcomes ($12, $8, and $4), and weight them according to the likelihood that they will occur. These weights are 80 percent, 10 percent, and 10 percent, respectively. The calculation is as follows:

$$\$12 \times 0.8 + \$8 \times 0.1 + \$4 \times 0.1 = \$10.80;$$

that is, the average of these outcomes is $10.80. In other words, assuming nothing changes in your range of possible interest rate movements, over time and by the law of averages you stand to increase your $10 stake by 80 cents each month. You also know that, in some months, thanks to adverse movements, you will lose money. But on average, the outcome of investing in this mutual fund will be positive.

What if you are worried not about the average outcome, but about a more subtle question: How much will potential outcomes vary around the average? This is known as the *variability* of the outcomes around the average and is often referred to as *variance*. It is calculated as follows:

$$0.8 \times (12 - 10.8)^2 + 0.1 \times (8 - 10.8)^2 + 0.1 \times (4 - 10.8)^2 = 6.55.$$

A further common measure of risk is known as *volatility*. It is the square root of variance—in this case, 2.56.

Some investors think that any investment that has a high variance or volatility is inherently risky. Unfortunately, reality is more complicated. For instance, it is intuitively obvious that Fund A offers you a good chance for an outcome that will be above average; any variability in this fund is skewed in the investor's favor.

To summarize, Fund A has a VaR of $6, a variance of 6.55, and a volatility of 2.56.

We now consider Fund B, a second mutual fund that has slightly different characteristics. From the same initial $10 stake, it will react differently to the same events (i.e., changes in interest rates), as shown in Figure 3.2.

This set of outcomes seems to have more symmetry (10, 80, 10) than those attached to Fund A; in other words, the outcomes are more evenly weighted in Fund B than in Fund A (see Figure 3.3). But a second glance reveals that the outcomes in Fund B are also heavily skewed on the downside. In fact, as most people can see intuitively, there is a 90 percent chance that you will lose $2 or more of your initial investment. By comparison, Fund A offered only a 20 percent chance that you might lose $2 or more.

Interestingly, some of the standard risk measures suggest that Fund B is less risky than Fund A. For instance, the volatility of Fund B is

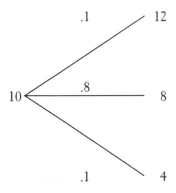

FIGURE 3.2 **Mark-to-future for Fund B.** The initial stake, $10, is to be invested for one month. Thanks to possible events, such as movements in interest rates, there is a 10 percent chance that the investment will rise to $12, an 80 percent chance that it will fall to $8, and a 10 percent chance that it will fall to $4.

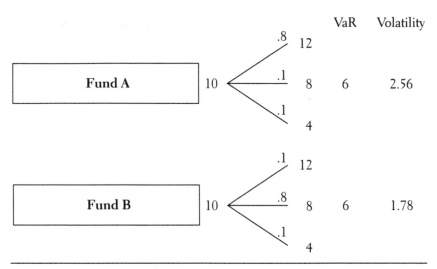

FIGURE 3.3   Mark-to-future for two funds. This diagram summarizes the mark-to-future for two notional funds, showing how our initial investment of $10 will fare under different scenarios.

lower than that of Fund A. Fund B has a mean outcome of $8 and a volatility of 1.78, whereas Fund A, as we know, has a mean outcome of $10.80 and a volatility of 2.56. Fund B has a lower volatility than Fund A. But curiously, Fund B has exactly the same VaR as Fund A: $6.

If you were to make your decision based on the two concepts of risk that are routinely used by professional mutual fund managers and banks—variance and VaR—you might prefer Fund B over Fund A.

This is despite the fact that Fund B looks intuitively riskier than Fund A; it has a far greater likelihood of delivering losses to its investors. So if you had $10, or $10,000, to allocate between these two funds, how would you decide between them, and in what proportion? Standard investment theory would suggest that you should put some money in each fund, with a larger amount going to Fund B. Yet most people would follow their intuition and put all of their money in Fund A because they can see the obvious skew in their favor it represents.

Positive skew is desirable; negative skew is not. Volatility or VaR might not capture skew and those who use these measures will lose the benefit that can be gained by looking at a Marking-to-Future result.

The fixed mathematics of volatility makes an assumption that is at odds with the real-world notion of skews. It assumes that the returns from Fund A are equally likely to be positive or negative. In other words, when you make an investment bet, the outcome will simply be either up or down. Hence, according to the formula, the higher its measured volatility, the less attractive an investment looks. In the real world, however, most portfolios and funds are skewed. There simply is none of the neat symmetry of outcomes implied by the volatility approach to risk.

To set the stage for a more realistic approach, let's consider a simple problem involving financial risk. To make our study interesting, we will choose a problem that has confounded financial theorists for some time. It is adapted from the work of Daniel Kahneman and Amos Tversky, two influential academics who conducted pioneering work in the field of behavioral psychology and cognitive science.

Assume you receive a $3,000 gift. Your broker offers to invest it in a fund and outlines the possibilities as follows. After one month, the $3,000 will either increase to $4,000, with a likelihood of 80 percent, or will be worth zero, with a 20 percent likelihood. Should you accept the offer or keep your $3,000 and wait for another opportunity? How should you analyze the problem? Figure 3.4 shows the problem in the form of a scenario diagram.

Another way of expressing this choice is in terms of the change in your position (Figure 3.5).

If you choose to accept the offer and, as a result, you lose everything, you will Regret the decision. If, on the other hand, you end up with $4,000, you will have no regrets. Is the $1,000 gain worth the extra risk you will assume? Does it offset the potential Regret of $3,000 you might experience? When this problem was posed to a large group

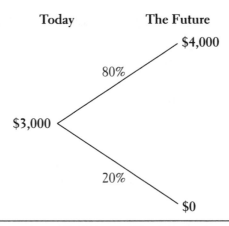

Today   **The Future**

80%
$3,000
20%

$4,000

$0

FIGURE 3.4   **Investing a $3,000 gift.** The initial value of your holdings is $3,000. If you invest it in the fund suggested by your broker, it may appreciate to $4,000 at some point in the future—or it may become worthless. The chance of it appreciating is 80 percent; the chance of it losing all its value is 20 percent.

of people, Kahneman and Tversky found that about 75 percent of the respondents would not have invested in the fund, and 25 percent said they would have invested.

Probability theory would instantly have you investing, because the average value of the bet is greater than $3,000. According to probability theory, the investment is worth 80 percent of $4,000, plus 20 percent of zero, which equals $3,200. This number, called the *expected value* or *mean*, is higher than the $3,000 you would have by not taking the investment. In other words, the odds are in your favor.

However, would most people value this offer at $3,200? Not according to the empirical results of Kahneman and Tversky.

The expected value is what you would observe if you were to make precisely the same choice hundreds of thousands of times. But it is not indicative of the value you should associate with the single choice facing you. Then how should one value this decision, which, despite its simplicity, is much like all investment decisions we have to make?

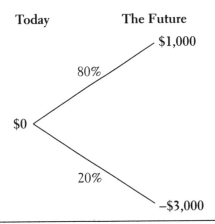

Today   **The Future**

                                             $1,000

                        80%

$0

                        20%

                                             −$3,000

FIGURE 3.5   Adventures of a $3,000 investment. This diagram shows the *change* in value of the $3,000 over time. The starting point—today—indicates $0, or no change. Change will occur only in the future. There is an 80 percent probability of gaining $1,000, because the investment could increase to $4,000 under this scenario. There is also a 20 percent chance that you could lose your entire investment of $3,000 if the second scenario occurs. The decision, therefore, as shown in the diagram, has an Upside of $1,000 and a Downside of $3,000.

A clue comes from the way in which we may place a value on a bet and the way in which we may value insurance. To distinguish these values, let's break the decision problem into two distinct parts: the upside and the downside. In valuing the upside, it may be helpful to think in terms of a bet; in valuing the downside, insurance may provide a model.

Imagine that you were offered a bet that would pay $1,000 and had a probability of 80 percent (Figure 3.6). How much is this bet worth to you? In other words, how much would you pay for the chance to participate in winning the $1,000? Very few people would choose to pay $800, which is the expected or average value and is therefore what probability theory would deem to be fair. In fact, few people would pay an amount even close to this value. (For proof, try out the opportunity on your friends.) You will probably find it difficult to get anybody to pay much

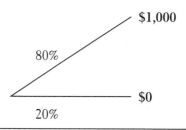

FIGURE 3.6   **The Upside.** There is an 80 percent chance of making $1,000.

more than $100 to take the bet. This amount—say it is $100—is the value of the upside to you. Different people will ascribe different values to such a bet, depending on their financial situation. A rich person is likely to pay more than a poor person for the same bet. If there were a market for such bets, with many participants, the market would ultimately come up with a fair price for the bet, which would be its objective value. In the absence of a market, the value is subjective.

We can value the downside (Figure 3.7) in a similar way, this time using insurance as the paradigm. Imagine that you were faced with a potential loss of $3,000, with 20 percent probability. How much, if anything, would you pay to insure against the loss? The richer you are, the more likely you are to self-insure—to pay nothing—because you can tolerate larger Regret. As with the upside, very few people would be willing to pay $600 (the expected value, 20 percent of $3,000) for this insurance. For the sake of argument, let's say you were willing to

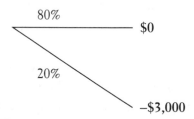

FIGURE 3.7   **The Downside.** There is a 20 percent chance of losing $3,000.

pay $120. This amount would then be your way of valuing the downside. If lots of people were simultaneously pricing this insurance, then there would be a market, and to obtain such insurance you would have to pay the market price.

By forcing you to place a value on the upside and downside of the investment, we are now able to give you a method for judging whether this is an investment you should make. The rule is simple. Subtract the cost of insuring the downside from the value of the upside. If the net result is positive, make the investment. If it is negative, don't invest. In the above example, the upside was valued at $100 and we were prepared to pay $120 to insure the downside. The difference is −$20.

We will call this value (upside value − cost of insuring the downside) the *risk-adjusted value* of the investment. A good investment has a positive risk-adjusted value. An investment with a negative risk-adjusted value should be avoided. We should avoid the above investment, based on the way in which we have valued the upside and downside. Its risk-adjusted value is −$20.

You will notice that different people will come up with different answers, based on their subjective assessment of the value of the upside bet and the downside insurance. If you believe that the insurance value of a potential loss of $3,000, with 20 percent likelihood, is only $80, then the risk-adjusted value of the investment would be $100 − $80 = $20. This is a positive number, and the investment should look attractive to you. This explains why some people would invest in this fund while others would not.

Kahneman and Tversky also considered the mirror image of this example in their experiment, to show that people react differently when they are already losing and could lose more. Once again, their empirical results show that, in two situations, which from a probabilistic or "rational" perspective are the same as far as the decision maker is concerned, people will react differently. People who are risk-averse in one situation turn into risk seekers in another, seemingly equivalent, situation.

In the mirror-image example, you are having a bad time. You have already lost $3,000. Then someone offers you an investment that could erase your loss, with 20 percent probability, or lose you an additional $1,000, with 80 percent probability. The expected value of the final position is −$3,200 (80 percent of −$4,000, plus 20 percent of zero).

Probability theory would point out that this amount is less than your starting position, so you should not invest. Yet empirical tests conducted by Kahneman and Tversky showed that most people would have invested. Why? (Notice that this "investment" is exactly the negative of the first situation we considered.) The scenario diagram for this situation is depicted in Figure 3.8.

Let's assume that the same person who valued the first investment applies consistent reasoning to valuing this one. In the first investment, the upside was $1,000, with 80 percent probability, and the downside was −$3,000, with 20 percent probability. We said that the person would

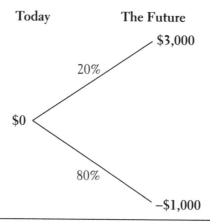

FIGURE 3.8 Further adventures of a $3,000 investment. This diagram shows the change relative to the $3,000 you are losing today. There is zero change ($0) today because change will occur only in the future if you invest in the fund. There is a 20 percent probability of gaining $3,000 (since the loss would be erased). There is also a 20 percent chance that you will lose $1,000 more if the second scenario occurs. This decision has an Upside of $3,000 and a Downside of − $1,000.

value the upside at $100 and the downside at −$120, giving a risk-adjusted value of −$20, so the decision was not to invest.

To be consistent, the same person should apply the same discount factors for the upside and downside in similar situations. *Discount factors* is another finance term that is more straightforward than language alone suggests. Before we can judge whether a value tomorrow is attractive to us, we have to know its value today. We also have to calculate tomorrow's value using a discount factor that reflects the time value of money—a dollar tomorrow is worth less than a dollar today. If we think the difference will be 10 percent, then we apply that to tomorrow's value to gain a figure that is equivalent to today's money.

In this case, our subject discounted the upside by $1/10 = $100/$1,000$ to get today's value, and discounted the downside by $1/25 = $120/$3,000$ to get today's value for the first investment problem. Applying the same logic here yields an upside value of $1/10 \times $3,000 = 300, and a downside value of $1/25 \times -$1,000 = -40. The risk-adjusted value of the second investment, consistent with the analysis done on the first investment, would be $300 − $40 = 260. This is a good investment, and the subject will take it. This outcome is entirely consistent with the findings of Kahneman and Tversky and entirely inconsistent with the assumptions of formal economics!

Another way of viewing these two examples from Kahneman and Tversky is to look at the uncertain payoffs of these two "deals" as being the payoffs facing the buyer and seller of a single deal (Figures 3.9 and 3.10).

On the face of it, the buyer gains when the seller loses and vice versa. This is sometimes referred to as a *zero sum game*. Why would two people enter into a deal like this, where the gain of one is the loss of the other? If the risk-adjusted value is negative for the buyer is it not positive for the seller? This would be a *lose–win* situation so you would expect one party always to shy away from the deal.

Wrong! There is a buyer and a seller in each deal, and each party believes the deal has a positive risk-adjusted value. That is, all deals are

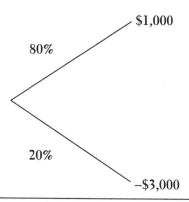

FIGURE 3.9 **The buyer's view.** There is an 80 percent chance the deal will pay $1,000. The downside is that, with a probability of 20 percent, the deal will lose $3,000.

win–win or else they would not be consummated. It is possible for deals to be win–win either because each party uses subjective assessments of the value of the upside and the cost of insuring the downside, *or* because the marginal effect of the deal on the individual portfolios leads to different marginal upside and downside amounts for each party. Even when there is only one market price for every level of upside and downside, it may still pay for two parties to trade!

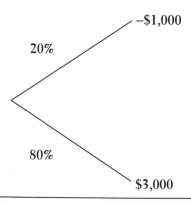

FIGURE 3.10 **The seller's view.** With a 20 percent chance, this deal could lose $1,000, but there is an 80 percent chance it could make $3,000.

In certain cases, such as investment decisions made in a mature market, the upside and downside can be priced objectively by finding portfolios with the exact same risk characteristics as the deal. In financial economics, this is known as a "complete market"—a market in which we can always find the exact combination of financial instruments to match any uncertain payoff we face. Suppose, for example, a lottery is being offered to the public. For an 80 percent chance of winning $1,000, the tickets are priced at $300. The upside would have a market (that is, objective) value of $300. If, in addition, an insurance company is prepared to sell you a policy costing $100 to cover you for a $3,000 loss, then the market value of the downside would be $100. The risk-adjusted value of the deal would therefore be $300 − $100 = $200.

Notice that the scenario diagram in Figure 3.11 looks much like the one we saw in Figure 3.9. In fact, it has the same payoffs, under the same conditions, with the same probabilities. So in the market we have described, where lotteries and insurance policies are available for the prices we have used, the risk-adjusted value of the deal is the true way in which it should be assessed. Today, if we could sell the right lottery ticket and buy the appropriate insurance policy, the payoff possibilities would be exactly the same as those in the deal we are evaluating. The lottery was worth $300 and the insurance policy could be bought for $100, so the net (risk-adjusted) value of the deal is $200. This is a good deal because the risk-adjusted value is positive.

For most investment decisions that we have to make, lotteries and insurance policies that exactly match the uncertain payoffs we face are not available. Instead, we need to make subjective estimates. Economists refer to this situation as an *incomplete market*—one in which not all scenario payoffs can be replicated.

Almost any choice that has financial consequences has an upside and a downside. If a choice were all downside, we would not enter into it voluntarily. If it were all upside, everybody would want to do it and it wouldn't last too long. The choice can be broken down into a

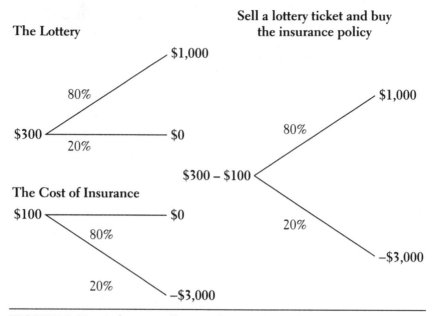

FIGURE 3.11   A theoretically complete market. The pending decision can be synthesized by selling the lottery (gain $300) and buying the insurance (cost $100).

bet (capturing the upside) and an insurance policy (capturing the downside). By accurately assessing the value of the bet and of the insurance policy to you today, you can arrive at a risk-adjusted value, which is a proper assessment of the true value of the deal. A positive risk-adjusted value means that the deal is in your favor and you should probably participate. It does not mean that you are certain to profit from the transaction. A negative risk-adjusted value means that the deal is biased and should be avoided. It does not mean you will definitely lose money if you enter the transaction. Using risk-adjusted valuation is simply a good and rational approach to financial transactions that have an uncertain future. As we have seen, risk-adjusted valuation is quite different from looking at the "fair," or average, or expected value based on probabilities. It is not a guarantee that all your decisions will be on the winning side!

Chapter 4

SWEET REGRET

I n light of the foregoing analysis, it seems that we need a better and broader measure of risk. The answer, we believe, is to adopt a concept known as *Regret*. (Astute readers will have noticed that we have slipped this term into several of our earlier discussions.) The power of Regret comes from the fact that it makes formal what we feel or know intuitively about particular decisions. Because our analysis of risk, unlike standard views, contains the concept of Regret, it does not assume either that there is symmetry of outcomes or that we all feel the same whichever outcome occurs. To begin to understand it, let us look again at Fund A, which we analyzed in Chapter 3. (See Figure 4.1.)

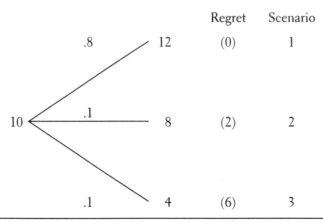

		Regret	Scenario
.8	12	(0)	1
.1	8	(2)	2
10			
.1	4	(6)	3

FIGURE 4.1 **Mark-to-future for Fund A.** One of these scenarios will occur in the future. If the first scenario occurs, you will have no Regret because the fund will have increased in value. If the second scenario occurs, your Regret will be 2 because your loss equals 2. Similarly, with the third scenario, Regret equals 6.

If interest rates rise, then, as an investor, you will have no Regret, for you have made money. If, on the other hand, rates stay the same, then you will have lost $2—an obvious cause of Regret. And if rates fall, you will clearly have more Regret than if rates simply stay the same. Your loss will be $6. Your benchmark for measuring how much Regret you will feel is the $10 you begin with (although, as we will see later, we could use another benchmark).

Because you do not know which of the three possible events will occur, it might help to calculate the average Regret on Fund A by multiplying each outcome by its probability of occurrence, and then dividing by the three outcomes. (We will see later that there might be better ways to "average out" over scenarios.) The answer is 0.8, so your average Regret with Fund A is a positive number. But it is also a small number. You will not have much Regret, even if the worst outcome occurs. You are not running a big downside risk.

By contrast, if Regret is a large number, then you are probably running a big risk of suffering very large losses. Fund B, by this measure, has a greater Regret than Fund A (Figure 4.2).

Put simply, Regret can be a measure of your potential average loss.

Add what you know about Regret to your earlier knowledge about volatility, and you have a richer information set on which to base an investment decision. In this case, it would lead you to prefer Fund A over Fund B.

Another way to view Regret—perhaps making it even more convincing as an ideal measure of risk—is by comparing it to insurance. Suppose you were able to purchase Fund A and simultaneously purchase insurance on the downside. If scenario 1 in Figure 4.1 were to occur, the fund increases in value and there is no need for insurance. If scenario 2 were to occur, the fund loses $2 (a drop from $10 to $8), and the insurance company would pay you $2. If scenario 3 were to occur, the loss is $6 (a drop from $10 to $4), and the insurance company would have to pay you $6. In other words, the payoffs match your

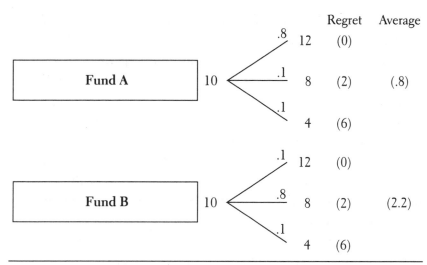

FIGURE 4.2 **Mark-to-future for Funds A and B.** The average Regret is obtained by multiplying the probability of the scenarios by the Regret value and summing up. Fund A has much less average Regret than Fund B. In this sense, it is less risky, because it would cost less to insure.

Regret in each scenario. We can then view Regret as equivalent to insuring the downside!

From this perspective, Regret is the amount of self-insurance we can tolerate. It represents a cutoff point below which we simply cannot bear the consequences of making a wrong decision, so we will go to great lengths to ascertain where our Regret point lies. Beyond Regret, our decision is more nuanced—our self-insurance vs. external insurance dilemma is defined by our appetite for risk, as we shall see later in the book.

The concept of Regret works in other contexts. Imagine that you have the opportunity to play in a simple, but fair, lottery. For a bet of $1, you stand to win either $1 million or nothing. Should you play? If you choose not to play, you keep your $1. If you decide to play, then your average return will be almost zero. On that basis alone, perhaps you would not play. The volatility of the lottery is extremely high, so you might also choose to avoid the wager. In short, just as with our two mutual funds, standard investment theory would tell you not to play this lottery.

However, with intuition as their guide, many—perhaps most—people would choose to play such a lottery. Why? Regret provides an explanation. Measured mathematically as well as practically, the Regret in this instance is minimal.

You will have a large upside if you win. And the potential upside is so high that you might even choose to forego eating a sandwich in order to play the lottery. If you lose, the loss would probably not break your personal bank. Even though the chances of winning are very small, the lottery has an outcome that is skewed in your favor because your downside is so small.

Imagine another lottery with exactly the same odds, but the prize has been raised to $10 billion and a single ticket costs $10,000. For many people, this would be a far more difficult proposition. For a person of modest means, it might be impossible to raise the stake. And for those who could stretch to raise the money, the Regret of losing would be much higher than in the first lottery, where the downside was almost inconsequential. Many people might therefore choose not to play.

However, those who can afford the stake might prefer to play the second lottery rather than the first, because the upside is so much bigger. In other words, they might choose to play the second lottery, even though, as losers, they would have higher Regret than if they played the first lottery. This is a clue to another important feature of Regret. How much Regret people feel varies, depending on their circumstances. Regret recognizes that the context in which choices are made is an important factor in determining why different people choose to act differently. It is sensitive to our unique circumstances.

Regret is not the same as disappointment. David Bell, a professor at Harvard, makes a neat distinction between the two. Imagine your boss has just called you in and told you that your reward for an excellent year's performance is a $5,000 bonus. Are you pleased? Yes; probably elated, especially if you were not expecting anything. But if you were expecting a $10,000 bonus, then you will be disappointed. In other words, your prior expectations will dictate how you feel. The higher your expectations, the greater the disappointment. Regret, says Professor Bell, is a psychological reaction to making a wrong decision where wrong is determined by actual outcomes rather than in relation to the information available at the time the decision was made. Put simply, if our benchmark for disappointment is our prior expectations, our benchmark for Regret is the outcome that would have resulted from a different choice. The stress here is on the *consequences of decisions* rather than on the *probabilities of particular outcomes*.

Is this distinction between Regret and disappointment really meaningful? Imagine a lottery that gives you a 50:50 chance of winning $0 or $10. If you play and lose, then you will feel disappointment. But if you chose the lottery over an alternative lottery that offered a sure $4, then you would feel both disappointment and Regret. (Interestingly, it is possible to suffer Regret without disappointment. This happens if the outcome of our choices exactly matches our expectations, but is less than we could have obtained from an alternative choice.)

Professor Bell also makes a neat distinction between risk and Regret that helps to explain why Regret is such a useful concept. Imagine that you regularly play a lottery and always pick the same combination of numbers. One week, out of boredom, you alter your numbers. You are still exposed to the same risk; your action has not changed the odds you face. However, you have exposed yourself to enormous Regret. Think how you would feel if your old numbers were to win in the very week you switched!

Decisions, Decisions

The idea of Regret has long been familiar to two types of economists whose interests overlap. Economists in the first group are known as "decision theorists." Decision theory has a long history. It is a field with close ties to risk management. How we decide things will, in part, be informed by our expectations of and appetites for the outcomes we anticipate from our chosen course of action. In economics, however, not all decision theory has been sensitive to risk management concerns. Indeed, economists have tended to be fixated on an abstraction—the so-called economic "agent" who is determined to maximize "utility" and makes decisions accordingly. (One of the failures of formal economics has been its use of jargon, but we hope the last sentence will be clear to most readers.)

In decision theory, the idea of Regret is used as a tool for formalizing the thought processes required when we face difficult decisions. Technically, these are known as *decisions under uncertainty*, a term that is at the very heart of our subject. We cannot predict the future, or even tomorrow, because it is uncertain. So how do we decide? We might try to consider the likely consequences for us in the event of particular outcomes (scenarios). Indeed, we might give greater weight to those potential consequences than we do to any probability-based assessment of likely outcomes.

George Shackle thought that we would be influenced by what he termed "potential surprise"—the nastier the surprise, the stronger our aversion to it. By making a telling observation, he attacked the idea that we should assign probabilities to possible outcomes as a basis for decisions. Assume that you think there will be three possible outcomes in the future, and you assign an equal one-third probability to each one. Then a surprise event occurs that raises the possibility of a fourth outcome. Does it suddenly make sense to alter the probabilities you have previously assigned to the other outcomes? If the answer is yes, then surely those original probabilities were wrong. Potential surprise is perhaps a different way of characterizing Regret.

How can we use Regret to help us make decisions? When governments make policy decisions, they have to weigh today's real costs against tomorrow's uncertain benefits. By attaching probabilities to future events (an act that changes uncertainty into risk), we can usually calculate what is known as our *net present benefit*, and use that as the basis for our decision. But if we know that there are many occasions when it is impossible to attach useful probabilities to an unknowable future, then we have to find ways to model the uncertainty we face.

Harry M. Markowitz, a Nobel laureate in economics, dealt neatly with the issue when he answered a question about retirement planning put to him by *Money* magazine. "I should have computed the historical co-variances of the asset classes and drawn an efficient frontier," he said. "Instead, I visualized my grief if the stock market went way up and I wasn't in it—or if it went way down and I was completely in it. My intention was to minimize my future regret. So I split my contributions fifty-fifty between bonds and equities."

A good example concerns the British government's preoccupation, during 1995 and 1996, with "mad cow disease" and the danger that it had mutated into forms that can infect humans. Even as we were writing this book in late 1997, the government banned the sale of beef on the bone, fearing the possible infection of consumers by a dementia-like condition. To many this seemed an extreme step, for the risk of infection appeared to be relatively small. (Ironically, around the same time the health authorities in Hong Kong ordered the slaughter of 1 million chickens because they feared that a small outbreak of a new form of influenza could become an epidemic.) How much should be done today to limit the future risk of a worse outbreak of the disease in humans? A big outbreak would represent a major public health disaster and could cost many billions to manage. However, taking all necessary steps now to eradicate the disease would certainly put a huge strain on public finances. This is particularly intriguing because politicians who decide policy suffer from a unique form of Regret—they can be blamed by voters either for acting or for not acting and booted out of office! Hence the occasional tendency to act, even if the risk appears relatively insignificant.

Here is how decision theorists use Regret when they approach such a problem. They begin by constructing a cost matrix like the one shown in Table 4.1. Simple arbitrary units are used to illustrate the point, but

TABLE 4.1
Assumptions about Infectivity (Scenarios)

	Zero	Low	Medium	High
Cost Matrix				
Do nothing	0	20	50	100
Mild intervention	10	20	35	60
Strong intervention	40	42	45	50

Source: *The Economist.*

real numbers can be substituted, particularly in a case that involves known scientific probabilities. The cost matrix lines up assumptions about whether humans will be infected, and rates them for three policy options: (1) do nothing; (2) undertake mild intervention in the form of selective culling of cattle; and (3) initiate strong intervention in the form of a complete cull of cattle. If the disease does not infect humans and the government does nothing, then its net cost is zero. It is assumed that the cost of mild intervention is 10, and strong intervention costs 40. That completes the first column of the matrix. To fill in the rows, start at the top by assuming that a low rate of infection will cost 20, a medium rate 50, and a high rate 100. The lower rows are completed by assuming that selective culling will reduce the likelihood of infection by 50 percent, and a total cull will reduce it by 90 percent.

Now the matrix can be used to guide our thinking. And we can thereby express our appetite for risk. If we are feeling lucky, we might choose the "minimim"—the minimum of minimums. Under this course, we would choose the policy that costs the least—in this case, the do-nothing option, which will cost us nothing if infectivity is zero. But it will cost us more than any other policy (i.e., 100) if the rate of infectivity is high. If, however, we are hypercautious, then we might choose the "minimax"—the minimum of maximums. For each policy, we ask what the worst result could be and then choose the policy that offers the best of these bad outcomes. The worst results are: for do nothing, 100; for mild intervention, 60; and for strong intervention, 50. We would choose strong intervention. This is the "best of a bad lot" philosophy.

This is where Regret comes in. Beginning with our cost matrix (Table 4.1), we can compile a Regret matrix (Table 4.2) by asking which policy produces the best result for each of the infectivity assumptions. Then we compare the results of the other two policies with that best result and we regard the difference in cost as a measure of our Regret. For example, the best result for medium infectivity is a cost of 35 from mild intervention. In our Regret matrix, that would be zero. The cost of doing nothing for medium infectivity is 50, so if we chose that policy we would be 50 − 35 worse off than if we chose the best policy; hence the 15 scored in that column in Table 4.2. The cost of strong intervention for medium infectivity is 45, so that scores 10 in our Regret matrix.

Now we can apply our minimax decision rules as before. For each policy, which outcome would we Regret most? For do nothing, the cost is 50 if infectivity turns out to be high. For mild intervention, the cost is 10 if infectivity turns out to be zero or high. And for strong intervention, the cost is 40 if infectivity turns out to be zero. Minimax Regret chooses the policy that gives the lowest of these results. In other words, it is not putting a floor under the disaster itself, but under how bad we are going to feel if things go wrong. In this case, we will choose mild intervention. This approach to decision making has not created

TABLE 4.2
Assumptions about Infectivity (with Regret)

	Zero	Low	Medium	High
Regret Matrix				
Do nothing	0	0	15	50
Mild intervention	10	0	0	10
Strong intervention	40	22	10	0

Source: *The Economist.*

certainty where none existed. But, thanks to Regret, it has created a structured way of thinking about an otherwise intractable problem.

Notice that, implicitly, we have used a very special benchmark: the "best possible" event under a given scenario. In this instance, we have invoked poetic license by using the word *Regret*. For decision theorists, this is the benchmark. We allow *any* benchmark when defining Regret.

Behaving Ourselves

A second group of economists is very familiar with the idea of Regret—the group known as *behavioral economists*. In essence, behavioral economists try to adapt standard economics and finance to take into account how people behave in the real world as opposed to the abstract world of pure theory. It is a controversial field, partly because it takes the normally dry domain of economics and stretches it into areas that are of widespread interest—psychology, for instance, and cognitive science. But it is also a richly rewarding field because its proponents are attempting to do something intuitively smart. They are trying to build models of economic behavior that capture more of the real world, with all its kinks and rough edges. We have already examined one famous experiment by Amos Tversky and Daniel Kahneman, two pioneers of behavioral economics.

To a behavioral economist, Regret is a concept that captures the frustration or despair we feel when bad things happen. Meir Statman, a leading professor in the field, offers the following example. Imagine that there are two identical roads that you can drive on to reach your home. Habitually, you take the high road. But one day, for no particular reason, you take the low road and you crash your car. Compare your reaction to how you would have felt if you had crashed on the normal road home. The higher sense of frustration you feel because you changed your routine is Regret.

Behavioral economists are intrigued by how feelings such as Regret affect people's behavior. For instance, many people have closed bank accounts in favor of investment accounts that function like ordinary checking accounts but allow liquid funds to be invested in the stock market. Often, holders of these accounts will defer writing a check because they want to keep their money exposed to the possibility of rising prices. They would feel Regret if they missed out on an upswing in the market.

People frequently make choices that appear strange. One of the most interesting aspects of behavioral economics is its efforts to understand "cognitive biases"—quirks in the way people think, which can lead them to do things that, on the surface, appear illogical, inconsistent, or just plain wrong-headed. Consider the difficulty we have in framing questions correctly so that we are divining useful answers. The average investor, for instance, probably knows nothing (or very little) about the central theories of modern finance. Those theories tell informed investors that they are unlikely to outperform the stock market on a consistent basis over time. But the vast majority of investors think, or at least hope, that what they choose to own will lead to superior performance— that they *can* beat the market. Why? If only logic were at work, many of these investors would be better off taking their money and investing it elsewhere, perhaps in tax-exempt bonds or an index fund.

The answer, according to behavioral economists such as Professor Statman, is that we are all affected by biases. "Most investors," says Statman, "simply cannot see that they are the suckers in the game. The real suckers are the ones who think they can divine inside information from the *Wall Street Journal.* For example, they might read an article about aging baby boomers who need bifocals and think they can make a buck by buying shares in an eyewear company. But they are usually just observing something that lots of other people already know."

Investors are often deceived by their tendency to frame basic questions wrongly. Consider the story about two hikers who are walking along a path and encounter a tiger. One turns to the other and says, "There's no point in running; that tiger is much faster than both of us."

"I disagree," replies the other. "The question is not how fast we are relative to the tiger, but whether I'm faster than you."

Suppose an investor wants to buy options on the Japanese yen. Professor Statman says the investor should ask: "What do I know about the yen, the trade deficit, and so on, that dozens of professional economists and currency traders don't know?" The answer would persuade most people not to make the investment. But people ask the wrong questions and go on investing because of an expectation that they might beat the market. As Professor Statman jokes, this phenomenon is probably the salvation of the market. Or, as Mark Twain once wrote: "Let us be thankful for the fools. But for them the rest of us could not succeed."

If these sound like abstractions, then consider the case of Microsoft Man, whose story appeared in *Grant's Interest Rate Observer*, a newsletter on financial markets. Microsoft Man worked in the computer industry. Before he became Microsoft Man, he owned a group of well-regarded and somewhat conservative mutual funds that had been assembled for him by a respected firm of money managers. Then one day he bought a few shares in Microsoft. The shares performed better than his mutual funds, so, one by one over a period of ten months, Microsoft Man sold all his funds and bought more and more shares in Microsoft. Finally, he owned only Microsoft shares, at which point the fund managers suggested that they no longer wanted his business. The newsletter remarked, in mid-1997: "To date, of course, he has had no cause for Regret."

Why might Microsoft Man suffer from Regret? Believing he knows better than his professional advisers do, he has broken a cardinal rule of finance theory by putting all of his eggs in a single basket. Assume Microsoft shares tumble at some point: our investor will suddenly find that his lack of diversification is extremely costly. At that point, he might remember the more balanced holdings he once owned. His Regret will be enormous.

Regret often creeps into everyday language. Alan Greenspan, chairman of America's Federal Reserve Bank, has an unenviable job: with his colleagues on the Federal Open Market Committee, he must set interest rates so that America's economy neither rushes into an inflationary boom nor collapses into a recession. This responsibility involves guessing (sorry; forecasting) where the economy is heading. Greenspan constantly peers into the future, trying to see the way ahead. When he testified before Congress in mid-1997, he used an analogy to describe the difficulty of operating in a world of uncertain forecasts: "A driver might tap the brakes to make sure not to be hit by a truck coming down the street, even if he thinks the chances of such an event are relatively low; the costs of being wrong are simply too high. Similarly, in conducting monetary policy, the Federal Reserve needs constantly to look down the road to gauge the future risks to the economy and act accordingly." Thus has Regret been officially endorsed by the world's top central banker!

We can gain more insight into Regret from other examples drawn from behavioral economics. Suppose you have bought two $100 tickets to a show at a theater that is a two-hour drive from your home. Just before you are due to set off, a nasty snowstorm begins. Driving will be hazardous. Do you make the trip? Most people would say yes; you have already spent $200, so you will make the effort. The $200 you have spent is a "sunk cost" that you are loath to sacrifice. But what if you had intended to buy tickets at the box office just before the show? You would feel far happier about not traveling. You would probably even turn down an offer to collect $200 if you make the trip. You feel far more comfortable about "losing" that $200 deal than you do about "losing" the same amount of money by not using tickets you had already bought. Or, in reverse, you would have far greater Regret if the storm caused you to miss the show when you had already bought tickets than if you passed up the chance to be paid $200 to attend the theater.

Regret also sheds light on the question of why people often behave like each other—they "follow the crowd." This phenomenon has been particularly evident in stock markets, where the tendency of investors to behave like a pack has often caused wild gyrations. Nowhere is this more true than in the United States. A generation of future retirees has poured money into stocks, pushing indexes such as the Dow Jones Industrial Average and the S&P 500 to ever new highs. Writers and commentators have tended to describe this behavior as irrational. Investors are said to be infected by manias that drive them into a frenzy of activity; then when reality dawns, the mania ends in a rush for the exit.

But what if Regret is at work? It is easy to see that many of us find some comfort from being in the same boat as others. Indeed, it is hard to find a genuine contrarian—someone truly prepared to go it alone and to live with the consequences (which can include ridicule). Perhaps we feel less Regret when we all fall together. If the stock market crashes, we might feel disappointment because our investment did not pay off, but we might feel only minimal Regret because millions of others will be suffering with us.

Even professional investors' behavior can be analyzed using Regret. It is well known, for instance, that fund managers like to do only a little better than their competitors, but hate to do either really well or really badly. Clients are suspicious of managers whose returns stray too far from the average. And when a fund manager takes a contrarian stance, the Regret can be enormous. In Britain, for example, one leading fund manager lost large amounts of assets under management after publicly expressing the view that it believed shares were wildly over-valued and switching toward bonds. That stance was not only wrong, but also exposed the firm in question to large Regret in the form of lost business. Other fund managers who watched this debacle probably felt it strengthen their intuition that it is best to be safely tucked in among the herd!

The same might be true of investment analysts, those highly paid experts whose job it is to assess the value of publicly traded companies. Only rarely does an analyst stick out her neck and issue a "sell" recommendation on a stock that is rated a "buy" by most of her peers. In addition to the flak that this can cause from the company concerned, the reason is simple. Her Regret for being wrong will be immense. It is much safer to be late and right than early and wrong!

No wonder traditional economists have a problem with behavioral economic analysis: it's fun!

Although they differ in how much weight they accord to human foibles, decision theorists and behavioral economists share a central concern about understanding how we make decisions—what motivates us, what scares us, what exhilarates us. And both are trying to face up to the tension between risk and uncertainty. If we rely too heavily on probabilities and "utility maximization" to guide our decisions, then we will likely end up suffering Regret. But in order to manage the risks that lie ahead of us, we must make attempts to reduce uncertainty. Regret recognizes that we care about the consequences of our decisions. Indeed, because each of us has a personal tolerance for Regret, some of us might sensibly weigh Regret more than we would chase the objective probabilities of a decision we face. In other words, if offered a bet with known probabilities, some of us might choose not to play because we could not stand the consequences of losing.

Although Regret has been discussed in economic and financial theory, it has never been placed at center stage in the way that we are seeking to promote it. However, we hope to show that it deserves a place among the key concepts of risk management and risk analysis. Regret can show us how our concern about downside risk (that is, losing money, or losing more money than we can afford) might guide us toward one choice over another, directing us toward investments that we feel intuitively more comfortable with than those that might be recommended by other commonly used "risk management" techniques such as mean variance and Value at Risk.

However, a really useful measure of risk is one that also takes into account potential upside returns (that is, making money!). We can now construct a range of scenarios showing the varying degrees of

Regret we would experience in each case. But how should we account for the expectation that we might also make more or less money within our scenarios? How do we reach a truly balanced view of our expectations about the future?

First, for the sake of argument, let's see how Regret itself, though an improvement on other techniques for measuring risk, can be imperfect. Figure 4.3 presents two portfolios that have the same Regret but quite different potential (upside) returns. (Incidentally, they have the same value-at-risk as well.)

How do we account for the fact that one portfolio has significantly better upside than the other, even though they both have the same Regret?

The answer lies in the fact that, acting like typical investors, we have separated the processes of how we measure risk and how we select our

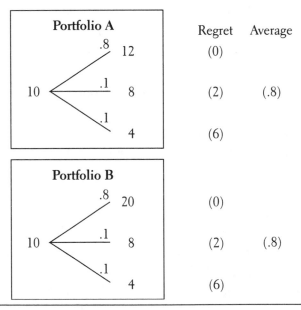

FIGURE 4.3 **Regret remains constant.** These two portfolios have significantly different potential returns, but the regret in each case is exactly the same.

investments. When we measure only risk, we usually think in terms of the downside—how we can avoid losses. But when we choose to invest in one stock or mutual fund, we focus primarily on our potential returns. We ask ourselves, "What is the upside, and how does it compare to what else is available?" However, we balance this query, implicitly or explicitly, with the potential for Regret. If we did not, we would simply put all our eggs in the best-looking basket.

Think what the separation of measurement and selection means. We give too much weight to Regret in the first instance, and too much weight to the upside in the second. This means that at the heart of our investment process are two mistakes—no wonder we are often surprised by the results of our decisions! Similarly, if we think of a business and how it allocates capital among its different operations, it should be obvious that a coherent system of risk management must include a unified approach to risk measurement and the selection of choices.

We have already argued that Regret is an improvement on traditional measures of risk. Can we go further? Yes; by developing a way to reconnect our measurement of risk with how we select portfolios or allocate capital. The necessary next step is to refine the notions of risk-adjusted return that we outlined previously. First, we need to make our description of Regret a little more formal. Figure 4.4 illustrates Regret by showing what it looks like for the simple choice we introduced in Chapter 3. At the center is the $10 we have today. The three points show the potential outcomes. Regret is the bold line that offsets the negative outcomes.

To calculate Regret, we take the following steps:

1. Subtract the benchmark from the portfolio value for each scenario outcome.
2. If it is negative (i.e., a loss with respect to the benchmark), then:
   a. Take the negative of this number (the negative of a negative is a positive); this is the Regret.

b. If the difference between the portfolio and the benchmark happens to be positive (i.e., again over the benchmark), then set the Regret to zero.

Measured over all scenarios that would cause losses, average Regret is the average of the difference between the chosen portfolio and the chosen benchmark. If the portfolio exceeds the benchmark, then we have no Regret. But if the portfolio underperforms the benchmark, we can measure the downside Regret. Any finance professionals who look at our picture of this downside exposure will see that the Regret function looks like a put option that has a maturity equal to the time horizon of our investment. In fact, if we could only price it correctly, that

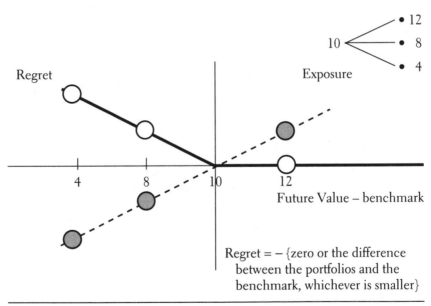

FIGURE 4.4 **Risk-adjusted return.** The black points on the tree diagram represent three potential outcomes for our initial stake of $10. In this example, our $10 is both the portfolio value today and the benchmark against which we measure the different outcomes.

put option would perfectly describe our Regret because it would cost the same as it should cost, in theory, to insure against the same level of downside risk.

(If you own a put option, it means that you can pass on a loss-making exposure to whoever sold you the option, so long as your losses occur within a specified period of time. For our purposes, the important point is that a put option neatly captures how we feel about insuring the downside. Similarly, a call option allows us to capture the upside.)

Notice that we have slipped into the idea of insurance again. In some circumstances, such as this one, risk and insurance are nearly equivalents. If we could take out an insurance policy against our downside risk, then the premium or price of that insurance ought to be the same as the price of a put option on that amount of losses. In effect, insurance can eliminate risk (with the proviso that we remain exposed to the insurer's ability to pay any claims). Thus, the cost of insurance should be equivalent to the value we need to place on the risk it eliminates.

Before we can go further, we need to introduce some ideas drawn from modern finance theory. One important idea has its origins in pioneering work in the 1950s by Merton Miller and Franco Modigliani on firms' capital structures—that is, the proportion of debt and equity firms hold—and whether they affect stock market values. Miller and Modigliani showed how, in a world without taxes, there is no optimal proportion of debt and equity that maximizes a firm's market value. If there were, then any divergence from the optimal level would swiftly be priced away by traders.

Merton Miller himself gives an amusing description of the "M&M theorem":

You understand the M&M theorem if you understand why this is a joke: The pizza delivery man comes to Yogi Berra after the game and says, "Yogi, how do you want this pizza cut, into quarters or eighths?" Yogi says, "Cut it into eight pieces, I'm feeling hungry tonight."

The joke is in the fact that the number and shape of the pieces doesn't affect the size of the pizza. Similarly, the stocks, bonds, warrants, etc., that have been issued don't affect the aggregate value of the firm. They just slice up the underlying earnings in different ways.

Miller and Modigliani went on to generate a host of related finance theories. One such development is central to our argument. To show that the stock market would price away any difference from some notionally optimal capital structure, the economists used the notion of "arbitrage." The simplest way to understand arbitrage is to go back to a time before computers and telephones sped up financial transactions. Savvy and well-equipped traders could monitor the price of gold in London and in Hong Kong, buying and selling in each place to exploit any small differences. In conducting this "temporal arbitrage," the traders would cause prices to fall back into line.

Other forms of arbitrage have now supplanted the temporal kind, largely because technology in the developed world has drastically reduced the time within which prices in two different physical locations can stray from parity. However, many finance theorists and economists have embraced an apparently peculiar idea: that we live in a world of "No Arbitrage." As Steve Ross, a leading financial economist at Yale, puts it, "That means there are no possibilities for true arbitrage in this stock market, in any of the markets, even underdeveloped markets. It is not possible to borrow at 10 percent and lend at 12 percent." How can this be? And isn't it equivalent to the joke about the economist who saw a $50 bill on the ground but refused to pick it up, insisting that it could not possibly be there because someone else would already have picked it up?

In actuality, the idea of No Arbitrage is not as crazy as it sounds — and it is very useful for our risk framework. In essence, it says that, for most participants in a market, there can be no arbitrage because any openings will have disappeared before they can react. Think about it.

If you are an investor, even a large one, what chance do you have of spotting and exploiting an arbitrage? Even assuming you can spot one, by the time you can act, market professionals will have forced prices back into line. And if there is a persistent anomaly, you run the risk that what you are entering is not an arbitrage but a price relationship that has incorporated new information and is therefore different.

For another way of thinking about No Arbitrage, imagine that you have two investment opportunities, each with a different interest rate. Once you adjust each opportunity for risk, then, in a world of No Arbitrage, the two opportunities are paying the same rate of interest. If you choose an investment that carries a higher interest rate, you are taking a risk relative to something with a lower interest rate.

Recall that Regret is equivalent to a put option on our downside exposure. To ensure that the option can be properly priced, we have to assume a world of No Arbitrage.

We have already noted that Regret as a downside measure is only half the picture. We also need to consider our potential Upside. Indeed, just as there is an expression for Regret, so there is one for Upside.

Instead of looking at the average for loss-making scenarios, we look at the average for those scenarios with Upside—in other words, where our portfolio outperforms the benchmark. Not surprisingly, given our earlier picture of downside Regret, Upside looks just like a "call" option on our net exposure, and has a maturity equal to our time horizon (Figure 4.5). All the future benefits we expect from owning this set of investments are captured by this option. In some sense, it represents the best we can do as owners of this portfolio. For that reason, it has interesting pricing characteristics. We won't value it higher than the Upside it represents, because that is the most it is worth. So we know the price of the call option that is Upside, and we know why we will not pay more than it is worth.

Upside is a powerfully seductive concept. Investors who look only at Upside and pay no regard to Regret have a dangerously tilted view of the world. Yet, thanks to the way fund managers are allowed to advertise

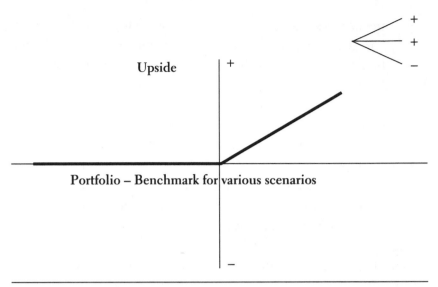

FIGURE 4.5   Portfolio minus benchmark for various scenarios. This figure of the Upside captures all the points at which our chosen portfolio outperforms our benchmark.

their performance, this is exactly what millions of people are encouraged to do. A glance at the advertisements in the financial press for mutual funds soon reveals that they are dominated by the Upside. Regret scarcely gets a look in.

What if we adopt an all-around view of our exposure by considering both Regret and Upside? We will then have a picture of our net performance, as follows:

U = Upside, which is equivalent to a call option on our future
    outperformance.

R = Downside (Regret), which is equivalent to insurance or a put option.

So long as U − R is a positive number, then we should want to hold the portfolio. We call this the *market value* of the deal. (When investment bankers talk of "marking a portfolio to market," they mean adjusting its value to reflect changes in market prices.) Put another way, if U is greater than R, then we should like the deal we are being offered because the Upside value is worth more than the cost of insuring the Downside. We should make more than we will lose.

Intuitively, we are always assessing such net exposures in our heads. Imagine you are offered a partnership in a law firm. Although you might not quantify the decision, you will almost certainly remember that your rewards (U) might be offset by the liabilities you will take on as a partner (R). These days, many directors of firms have to weigh their share options (U) against the danger that they might be subjected to a shareholder lawsuit (R). Firms can make directorships more attractive by protecting against Regret via directors' insurance.

Measuring Our Hunger for Risk

We have argued that the concepts of Regret and Upside greatly improve our ability to think coherently about risk. We have also asserted that Regret is more useful than existing risk measures because it can reflect our appetites for risk. We need to explore in more detail how this works in practice. To do that, we introduce the concept of risk-adjusted value—value that has been altered to take into account our personal attitude toward risk. We are more prone to risk in some circumstances than in others. To reflect these differences in our behavior, we introduce a *risk aversion constant* we designate as lambda (λ), the eleventh letter of the Greek alphabet.

The risk-adjusted value of a deal is then $U - \lambda R$. This translates as: the upside minus lambda (the risk-adjusted constant) times the downside or Regret. Lambda typically is greater than 1 because we usually are risk-averse.

Another way to think of lambda is as a margin or insurance premium that we might decide to put aside against our possible losses, in the event that our Upside fails to materialize. The larger the value for lambda, the more risk-averse the decision maker, because he or she is paying a higher price to self-insure the risk. People who only take the risk into account when making a deal essentially have a very high lambda. Typically, lambda is greater than 1; otherwise, we are, in effect, paying less than the cost of insurance to cover the risk, and will not be adequately covered. Another way of saying this is that most people would like to have the assurance that they've set aside sufficient funds to protect their downside. Most of us are risk averse! On the other hand, when a decision is largely based on the Upside, the decision maker discounts risk with a very small lambda. If the impact of our lambda is less than 1, then we would be paying our counterparty for the privilege of taking on risk, something that happens occasionally when we feel especially bullish. We might then be referred to as risk seekers.

Why does this mental exercise help us to reach a better way of valuing risky decisions?

Most of us, following the coaching of investment advisers, have split our funds in a pyramid fashion, with a small portion going to risky investments (low lambda), a larger portion going to mutual funds (medium lambda), and the bulk placed in safe investments such as bonds (high lambda). In effect, we set the lambda for each portion of our holdings and purchase the best available investments for each portion. That is, we seek the investments that maximize the risk-adjusted value $(U - \lambda R)$ for that portion of the fund.

A valuable concept is that of the *Implied lambda*. Once we know that a deal has been done, it is easy to work out the implied risk appetite of the counterparties. Assume we observe execution of a deal where the Upside is equal to U and Regret is equal to R. It must mean that the decision maker has placed a positive value on $(U - \lambda R)$. Therefore, the allowance she has made for risk aversion (lambda) must be less than the Upside divided by Regret.

A natural framework, analogous to the No Arbitrage framework of finance mentioned earlier, assumes that each risky deal that is executed, or each decision involving risk that is acted on, only happens when the outcome is "win–win" for both sides of the deal. (For more on win–win contracts, see Chapter 7.) In other words, each party must be viewing the deal as having positive risk-adjusted value, or else they would not enter into it. Thus, each party has $U - \lambda R$ greater than 0.

An Implied lambda is another way of expressing the same fact. We can solve the above equation and find the party's Implied lambda — that is, the risk aversion constant that he or she had to have assumed in order to go ahead with the deal. In complete markets, U and R are unique and thus the same for both parties. In incomplete markets, as we saw earlier, each party might have a different value for U and R.

In a complete market, one party's Regret is another party's Upside, and vice versa. If there are two parties, A and B, then:

$$\lambda A \text{ less than } U/R \text{ and } \lambda B \text{ less than } R/U$$

for the deal to be win–win. This, in turn, means that one party must be a risk taker and the other a risk avoider with respect to this single deal. However, people hardly ever make deals in isolation. Any individual deal will be measured for its effect on the Upside and Regret of the deal maker's *overall* holdings. If the deal improves the risk-adjusted value of the entire portfolio, then it is a good deal.

This portfolio effect is one of the most important features of financial and business risk. It explains why some people can afford deals that others cannot. It also explains why many transactions that might seem uneconomic can occur in the real world. Where one party holds a portfolio which contains an offsetting position or asset, it is possible to conduct business that benefits both parties. Often we overlook the portfolio dimension of our decisions. This can result in the systematic mis-pricing of deals and, consequently, poor risk management.

To begin to understand the power of lambda, think of how we select a mutual fund today. Assume that we wish to choose from the very best funds appropriate to investment needs. As we will see in a subsequent chapter, we need lots of information before we can make an informed choice, but remarkably little useful information is available. However, let's assume for the moment that we want a single number that will indicate how we might choose among a small number of options.

What data are available to inform our choice today? Typically, we are offered two tidbits of information. The first tells us a fund's absolute performance over the past year—a simple 12-month percentage of total return. The second gives us a measure of the fund's return against its chosen benchmark (known as beta, this tells how much the fund has fluctuated compared to its benchmark); in short, we know how volatile the fund has been relative to its peers.

Both of these numbers are historical—they show us how the fund has performed in the recent past. But we know intuitively that a proper measure of risk looks forward rather than backward. As explained in Chapter 1, when we think about managing risk, we know that it is foolish to assume that history alone is a good predictor of the future.

Using modern risk management and Regret, a particular investment option can look different depending on your appetite for risk, provided the latter takes into account both your downside aversion and your upside hopes. To illustrate this, let us look at how we might choose among competing mutual funds.

Imagine three rival funds that we have determined are the best in their class:

Fund A has an expected upside of $10 and a possible downside of $5.

Fund B has an expected upside of $30 and a possible downside of $40.

Fund C has an expected upside of $15 and a possible downside of $5.

How might we select among these funds? The power of our U − R (risk-adjusted) analysis is that it recognizes our intuition: we feel differently about particular choices, depending on the relative weights we place on the upside and the downside—in other words, how risky we think the world is. The greater our tolerance for risk, the less attention we will pay to the downside. If we are assessing a mutual fund as a potential element in our stable of speculative investments, we will be relatively unconcerned about events that might cause large temporary losses. But if the fund is to be part of our core, long-term holdings, we will place correspondingly more stress on downside risk. We will give lambda a high value because we will be biased against funds with big downside risk.

Incidentally, the above paragraph contains a classic example of what behavioral economists call "framing." Can you spot it? (The answer is at the end of the chapter on page 106.)

Let us assign to lambda three values that reflect varying attitudes toward risk. The higher the value, the more we feel disinclined to take on risk:

1. We actively seek risk. $\lambda = 0.2$
2. We are neutral. $\lambda = 1$
3. We are very risk averse. $\lambda = 5$

Now, we apply each value of lambda to each of our potential choices of funds (see Table 4.3).

If we are risk averse ($\lambda = 5$), we will tend to avoid Fund B. Even though it has the greatest potential upside, it has the probability of large Regret (\$ −170). In fact, we will greatly prefer Fund C because it has the highest risk-adjusted value (\$ −10). Fund A also gives off a powerful signal that its downside risk is significant in relation to its potential upside.

TABLE 4.3
Risk-Adjusted Valuation for Three Funds

		Expected Upside		Possible Downside		Value of Lambda		Adjusted Value
Fund A	1.	$10	–	($5	×	0.2)	=	$ 9
	2.	10	–	(5	×	1	=	5
	3.	10	–	(5	×	5)	=	–25
Fund B	1.	$30	–	($40	×	0.2)	=	$ 22
	2.	30	–	(40	×	1)	=	–10
	3.	30	–	(40	×	5)	=	–170
Fund C	1.	$15	–	($5	×	0.2)	=	$ 14
	2.	15	–	(5	×	1)	=	10
	3.	15	–	(5	×	5)	=	–10

If our attitude toward risk is neutral, then we might choose Fund C. Its upside is closely mirrored by its downside—our expectation of a positive return is offset by the possibility of an equal loss. But the extent of the potential loss is limited; hence our relative lack of concern.

If we are actively seeking risk and will give greater weight to our potential return than to our possible losses, lambda will lead us to Fund B.

If we can use lambda to help us choose among three funds, depending on our tolerance for risk, then there seems little practical barrier against using lambda as a general means of making relative rather than absolute choices pertaining to risk. We can use lambda, for example, to judge whether we have sufficient margin/capital to cover losses in a worst-case scenario. Nicholas Leeson of Barings was allowed to run up losses that exceeded his bank's entire capital. Most banks have "trading limits"—in theory, no one person or trading desk is given sufficient scope that its risk taking might endanger the bank's solvency. It is a sensible rule of thumb that an operation should not take on positions that expose it to the worst possible outcome—that a catastrophic loss might occur, resulting in ruin. The same applies to an investor who is concerned about avoiding unaffordable losses. Trading limits based on historical estimates of risk exposure will not be adequate.

If we think of the tree scenario diagram, the analogy would be that we need to prune those branches where Regret is higher than we can tolerate—we need to insure ourselves against the worst, the maximum Regret. Once we have done that, we can set our risk limits within the remaining scenarios. If we were a bank, for example, we would have a separate threshold for Regret once we had eliminated those exposures that are unacceptable to us. This threshold would be the basis for operating decisions on, say, trading limits.

Another useful example is to think of those now infamous "Names," many of whom lost their homes and ruined their lives in the mid-1990s after they signed up as members of underwriting syndicates at Lloyd's of London, the world's biggest insurance market. Some Names were unlucky in that they were the victims of fraud—they were rudely assigned all the worst risks in the market by insiders who were keeping the best risks for themselves and a few favored customers. Many more Names, however, made a disastrous risk management decision which, if only they had had a simple tool such as lambda, they might have avoided. The essence of their mistake was that they gave too little weight to the risk that, in signing up at Lloyd's, they agreed to unlimited downside exposure in return for an uncertain annual income. While markets prospered, the downside risk barely registered, and the checks flowed with soothing regularity. But the life-destroying effects became all too evident when Lloyd's ran into problems. Some were self-inflicted, but others were caused by the normal cyclical changes that the insurance industry experiences.

Now think back to a Name's moment of decision—to sign up or pass the deal by? Using an approach based on Regret and lambda, a would-be Name would have quickly seen that he or she should assign a large value for lambda to the risk of total loss, even if it was thought unlikely that such a loss would ever be faced. This simple step might have saved hundreds of middle-class investors from ruin, just by bringing to their attention the possibility that they could end up homeless and penniless. Instead, they were seduced by what they thought was the happy Upside of belonging to the world's leading insurance market. A technique such as applying lambda makes it very clear that, under the market structure as it then existed, the role of a Name at Lloyd's was only for the extremely wealthy or those with very large liquid assets who could afford to pay out hefty cash sums when required to do so. Even some very wealthy investors were caught out by Lloyd's, so large was the cash amount required to cover its multibillion-dollar losses. Aristocrats dislike having to sell the family castle in order to raise cash, even though, unlike the rest of us, they might not be ruined by the act!

The same thinking applies to a decision most of us face at one time or another: Should we buy a house? Plenty of examples show that this decision is fraught with risk. For instance, in 1981, the Toronto housing market was going crazy. Interest rates were 14 percent, but house prices had been rising steadily for five years and seemed to be accelerating. So one cash-strapped would-be buyer made an apparently rational calculation: borrow a large amount at favorable short-term rates, buy a wreck of a house and renovate it, then sell it for a profit and repay the loan, or keep the now more valuable house and refinance the loan into a relatively small long-term mortgage. What could go wrong?

Everything, it turned out. First, interest rates jumped to nearly 24 percent in the space of six months, so borrowed short-term cash suddenly became very expensive. Second, the renovations took longer than planned, so refinancing was not an option. Third, house prices began to tumble, so the expected equity gains did not materialize. This particular bankrupt buyer was bailed out by a family member and was able to keep the house. But the Regret suffered (not to mention the ulcers that grew during the struggle to stay afloat) was palpable.

This buyer would have done better if she had examined her assumptions about interest rates and the housing market. If rates rose, it was highly likely that house prices would come off the boil. Moreover, the carrying cost of a big short-term loan would jump. Either or both of these scenarios would be painful. But the pain could instantly have been mitigated. If financing had been locked in at the outset, our buyer would have been largely indifferent to future changes in interest rates. True, falling house prices might dent assumptions about when the wreck would be worth $1 million! But, living under a secure roof, our buyer would have had time to spare for renovations.

Now let's move to England in 1989. Our subject is a naturally cautious bank clerk who is keen to move into his own apartment. Again, the housing market is in full bubble mode. Prices are rising effortlessly and quickly. Would-be buyers are desperately competing to buy almost anything, on the grounds that it can only be worth more in the future and will thus be the basis on which they can "trade up" for something bigger. Our clerk could rent a place. But funding a mortgage will be cheaper in the short term, thanks to low interest rates. So he opts for independence and decides to enter the market. He has only a small salary, so his ability to borrow is limited. He must put down all of his savings in order to secure a mortgage. For the equivalent of $75,000, he buys a studio apartment in a thoroughly unfashionable London district. After putting $20,000 down, he must finance a $55,000 mortgage. But rising house prices will surely make the deal look good before long. And even if prices were to fall a little, the $20,000 deposit looks like an adequate cushion. What can go wrong?

Everything. As the British economy began to deteriorate in 1990 and 1991, the housing market came sharply off the boil. Prices fell across the board. But they fell especially hard at the bottom of the market. Studio apartments had been created by the thousands, by developers with keen noses for a quick buck. Suddenly, there was no demand for them, so the prospective chain of "trading up" simply disappeared. First-time buyers withdrew, fearing that they would instantly lose money in a falling market.

Our conservative bank clerk was hit particularly hard. His apartment collapsed in value. At the bottom of the market in 1995, it was valued at around $35,000, or $20,000 less than the mortgage. With all deposit equity lost, the clerk was forced to approach his lender. Having been offered a new job in a city far to the north of London, he wanted desperately to sell the apartment. But no one was willing to buy what suddenly looked like an overpriced room in a run-down suburb. The only solution was hugely costly. He had to rent out the apartment at a loss, in order to take the new job. Eventually, he sold the property at a thumping loss, refinanced his remaining mortgage, agreed to pay off a personal loan in addition, and finally cleared his debt five years after assuming it.

Such "negative equity" scared and hurt a generation of British house buyers, many of them young and ill-equipped to bear the financial shock. Indeed, as we write this book, it is remarkable that a new house-price bubble is underway in Britain. Have those who were so badly burned forgotten the lesson that prices do not rise forever? Think of our clerk. If he had paid the little extra to rent for a while, he would still have his $20,000 savings and might have used this money to fund a more sensible purchase when prices became more affordable. In retrospect, his Regret from entering the market was enormous. His financial position literally will never be the same.

In both of our examples, hindsight is everything. There are plenty of cases where people have stayed out of housing markets only to see prices rise anyway. Someone who bought an apartment in New York in 1994, for instance, would have made a fat return in the space of three years. Someone who rented over the same period merely faced escalating rents!

Here is the answer to the framing question on page 101: Look at the sentences about our different attitude toward the two mutual funds. They assume that in our brains we have "boxes" or "layers" into which we assign different categories of risk—one box for safety-first, another for risky stuff, and so on. We would have less Regret if a fund we know to be highly risky were to underperform so that we lost money, than if a fund we thought was safe produced losses instead. But, as behavioral economists would jump to point out, by assigning different risks to mental boxes or layers, we risk falling into a classic error—we ignore the portfolio effects of holding sets of funds. This is, by the way, a common mistake among investors. How all of the assets we hold interrelate with each other (the finance term for this is covariance) is crucial to our ability to construct efficient portfolios.

Kenneth Fisher, who runs an investment firm in California, has pointed out the term investment is derived from the Latin word vestiment, meaning clothes or layers. Investment, then, means covering oneself with layers. Perhaps in view of our Regret analysis, the term might be limited to covering a particular part of one's anatomy!

Chapter 5

KEEPING UP WITH
THE JONESES

I magine you inherit a modest cash sum, say $5,000. What should you do with the money? If you put it in an envelope and hide it under your roof, your cash might be safe, but its value would be eroded by inflation, so you would risk having a smaller amount of real spending power in the future. You could deposit your money in a bank, earning a nominal amount of interest that might offset the effects of inflation. Alternatively, you could place the money in a mutual fund and hope to see the capital sum grow much faster than inflation. And if you were really aggressive, you might visit a casino and try to double your money on a single bet at roulette.

How will you think about this decision? For one thing, you will always have a base case in mind—doing nothing, opening a bank account, or investing in a mutual fund. That choice will help to determine how you feel about the alternatives. If you choose opening a bank account as your base case, you will set that choice as a benchmark against which you will measure alternative outcomes. By this measure, if you then sneak off to the casino and lose your money, you will have underperformed!

We make comparisons constantly, whether with neighbors, colleagues, or business partners. Often, money is a simple benchmark—we weigh the price of one thing against the price of another, using money as the metric. That is why we go to such trouble to measure inflation and foreign currency rates. We need to know how the value of money is changing before we can use it as a benchmark.

But we use many other benchmarks. When we buy a washing machine, money forms one benchmark, but we might also look at consumer surveys that rank machines according to their reliability and economy. We also apply aesthetic benchmarks. Some people like garish carpets that, to others, are the epitome of vulgar taste. Is your child behaving well? It depends in part on the behavior permitted in the past, as well as on the context. Fixed rules are one thing, but they are unenforceable if other children are operating under different rules and your child is on a playdate at their house. In this case, a parent might shift the benchmark, at least until the child gets home!

How we feel about our experiences may be determined by our benchmarks. But the result can be highly subjective behavior. When on vacation, for instance, we might feel let down by one tour because our benchmark is a wonderful, but more expensive, trip that we took two years earlier. When we sulk because colleagues have been awarded merit increases to their pay, we reject whatever benchmark led our boss to overlook us. When we buy a car, our satisfaction might be lessened if it develops more engine problems than our neighbor's less expensive model.

Cars provide an excellent example of how we use benchmarks in complex ways in everyday life. When we visit a Cadillac dealer, we will be comparing the showroom models with those on display down the road at the rival Lexus dealership. We will almost certainly not compare a Cadillac with a Volkswagen or a Ford Taurus. At a general level, we seek comparable cars and weigh their comparable characteristics.

Then things become a little more complicated. We assess the car's selling points and weigh these in our minds. How fast can it accelerate? What is its fuel consumption? What will its resale value be two years from now? What is its safety record? Will it impress our friends? In effect, we give a weight to each factor as we assess a car. And we compare the total weight to notional ideal weightings—our benchmark. If the Cadillac scores well enough, then we will feel happy about buying it. But if, for instance, it scores poorly because it is relatively slow to accelerate, then we might reject it in favor of a Porsche or a Saab. People have many different ways of approaching a major purchase such as a car. It is remarkably common to find a high degree of quantitative analysis in the process by which we form our own highly personal benchmarks. In effect, we add various factors together and construct our own index for use as our benchmark. It is also very common for people to use a published index of some kind as a benchmark.

Car manufacturers and dealers are well aware of (and try to exploit) how we use benchmarks. Since the 1980s, Japanese cars, especially Toyotas, have become widely used benchmarks among consumers because they represent a good combination of price and quality. Now some American firms openly compare their cars with similar Toyota models, and they urge consumers not to dismiss less fancied lines. One New York dealer went so far as to place the rival cars side by side, arguing that this is what customers would do in their minds anyway. Advertisers also try, in more subtle ways, to exploit how we use benchmarks. Some people like the idea of owning a best-selling car, so that is a sensible pitch for Ford, which dominates the mass market. Ford owners might give this factor a high weighting. Other drivers, however, would rather walk than drive a Taurus. They give a high weighting to standing out from the crowd. Some cars are therefore positioned as quirky. In America, for instance, advertising for Saab explicitly appeals to the urge to escape anonymity. Potential buyers are advised to "find your own road." Owning one of these cars is represented as a powerful statement of individuality and confidence.

Advertising in general is an attempt by firms to do one of two things. The chief objective is to establish products and services as benchmarks, so that consumers mentally use them as the basis for their comparisons. But another important objective is to alter people's risk-adjusted calculations, either by increasing their sense of Upside ("You will be a better person if you [drink this cola] or [buy mutual funds through this broker]"), or by decreasing their sense of Regret ("Buy SunAmerica's retirement plan and you will have a more secure old age"). If an advertiser can tweak our attitude sufficiently, it can alter our risk-adjusted view so that we will accept or buy something we otherwise would reject.

By becoming an accepted benchmark, a product such as a car can acquire a potent market position. The same is true of many consumer goods. Think of how many millions are spent promoting brands of all kinds. The underlying rationale for this spending is that a leading brand creates unusual value because it is used by consumers as a benchmark. But, as Toyota has learned, there is no permanent comfort in being a benchmark. At the very least, other firms can use a rival's benchmark position to pitch prices that appeal to consumers: "Why buy the leading brand when you can buy brand X for half the price?"

It is vital that we choose the right benchmarks. Otherwise, we will continually be puzzled and disappointed by our performance and experience. If we live in London, there is little point in comparing the price of our house to apartment prices in Tokyo. Instead, the correct benchmark is the relative performance of other houses in our neighborhood and of houses in other neighborhoods. If our house is keeping pace, then we are performing in line with our benchmark. But our circumstances might change. If we consider moving to the countryside because our house has sharply increased in value relative to country houses, then we are changing our benchmark to reflect our new focus. And if our company asked us to relocate to Tokyo, we would acquire a valid interest in apartment prices there. We would change our benchmark to reflect our scenarios.

Similarly, if we are running a dry cleaning company in Toronto, we will set our benchmark for staff salaries according to local rates. We don't care that New York dry cleaners earn three times as much; most of our workers are not in a position to move there. If we are running a software firm, however, our benchmark cannot focus purely on local factors. We need to incorporate a weighting that recognizes a going rate for top programmers wherever they are. Otherwise, we run the risk of losing our best employees. This is true in any business where skills are easily transferable.

If we set the wrong benchmark, we will invariably behave foolishly. A manufacturing firm might build a factory in the riskier of two new markets if its benchmark is the return it might otherwise earn by investing in high-risk shares. With a more appropriate benchmark, it might decide to build in the safer market. An oil company would never think twice about sinking another well if its benchmark was the return on cash—the potential returns would always argue in favor of more exploration. A benchmark that is set too high will encourage us to take risks that will lead to Regret. But a benchmark set too low is useless because almost anything will look good by comparison.

Getting It Right

If this all seems straightforward, perhaps it is. However, it is surprising to find that life and business are riddled with examples of muddle and misunderstanding about benchmarks. Take the problem of measuring mutual funds' performance. Several firms offer performance rankings that purport to reflect the risk taken by each fund. Perhaps the best known among such rankings are the coveted stars awarded by Morningstar. A five-star ranking is almost a guarantee that investors will flock to a fund. Open any day's *Wall Street Journal* and you will see advertisements for top-ranked funds. And if you look carefully, you find some small print that funds place at the bottom of their ads.

As an example, we chose at random, from myriad possibilities, a Franklin growth fund. The small print is as follows:

Morningstar ratings are calculated from the fund's three-, five-, and ten-year average annual returns in excess of 90-day Treasury bill returns with appropriate sales charge adjustments, and a risk factor that reflects fund performance below 90-day T-bill returns.

The catch is in the last phrase. Morningstar's benchmark for equity funds' downside risk is three-month government bonds. The reason for the choice is clear: these are seen as a useful proxy for the risk-free rate of return, or what you should earn on your money by assuming almost no risk. How useful is this information? Although there can be long periods when changes in short-term interest rates cause the stock and bond markets to move in the same direction, there can be other periods when this does not happen. Interest rates could be affecting bonds and shares quite differently. But an investor who looks at Morningstar stars for advice on equity funds has no idea that the benchmark may be utterly unhelpful.

Many companies show a basic misunderstanding of benchmarks when they announce that they intend to measure their performance with reference to a "hurdle rate"—a rate of return that they hope to make from their ongoing operations, and, often, the minimum level required before they will invest in a new project. This hurdle rate is often chosen arbitrarily. If the current rate of return on Treasury bills is 5 percent, firms will announce and stick with a hurdle rate of 8 percent, arguing that the 3 percent is the extra reward investors earn for the greater risks inherent in their shares.

There are glaring flaws in this approach. First, many businesses are cyclical—their profits swing wildly, depending on the economic conditions faced by their industry. An unchanging benchmark will almost guarantee a misleading picture of how these businesses have actually performed. If the hurdle rate is 8 percent and a paper firm earns 20 percent, then investors might think that the firm's managers have done a wonderful job. If that return is earned at the top of the cycle, however, 8 percent is a woeful benchmark. It is possible that the managers have only performed as well as they should have, given the economic conditions. And it is possible that they have actually underperformed their peers in the industry. A rate of return over an entire economic cycle might be a good measure of a firm's performance. In that case, managers should make a point of underplaying high returns at the top of the cycle, just as they often try to downplay low or negative returns when conditions are less favorable.

What happens if interest rates change? Under one interest-rate scenario, a fixed hurdle rate might look very silly indeed. Under another scenario, it could appear highly risky.

A sound approach to benchmarks recognizes that, just as a firm's performance will depend on the scenarios it encounters, so a benchmark's performance is "scenario-dependent." A well-chosen benchmark should be subject to the same or similar scenarios as its point of comparison. To extend the example above, because our paper firm's earnings will swing in some relationship to the price of its raw materials, the gyrations of pulp prices might be an appropriate benchmark for the firm's gyrating earnings. If the firm chooses to smooth out some of those gyrations by locking in the prices at which it buys pulp in the future, then its reference point might still properly be the underlying gyrations. The cost of its intervention would be the cost its managers incur by departing from the benchmark. When they buy insurance, they are guaranteeing that their performance will deviate from that of the benchmark.

A second flaw in the hurdle rate approach is precisely its lack of scenario dependency. An 8 percent rate of return has no intrinsic relationship with the thing it is supposed to be measuring. For a multinational firm, 8 percent might be the perfect benchmark in a stable and mature economy. But in a volatile and immature economy, the firm might need a significantly higher benchmark that reflects the different scenarios it faces. People often fail to realize that a benchmark itself captures certain behavior. If you choose the average of the Standard & Poor's 500 index as a benchmark, its performance will reflect the aggregate behavior of its constituent parts. It is an appropriate benchmark if you want to measure how well a broad-based portfolio of industrial shares has performed, because the affecting factors are largely similar. It is a lousy benchmark if you own a portfolio of tax-exempt bonds. It is an appropriate benchmark if it matches your appetite for risk, but a lousy one if you are highly risk averse.

The idea that benchmarks themselves capture a set of risks may be difficult to grasp, but is quite logical. When we choose a benchmark, a vital question is: Does it accurately reflect our risk appetite and our return goals? A central argument of this book is that our choice of benchmark is one of the few things we can actively manage in an uncertain world. When we try to see tomorrow, we need to do so from the correct (and perhaps unique) perspective of a well-chosen benchmark. Otherwise, we are certain to make mistakes.

Our difficulties with benchmarks help to explain an enduring mystery of financial markets. Big pension funds often make a basic risk management mistake when they appoint fund managers. It is common practice to measure managers' performance against an index (preferably one that reflects the chosen manager's investment style)—and against the managers' professional rivals. An entire industry has grown up to track fund managers against indexes and each other. However, few pension funds have questioned whether these benchmarks make sense. Often, because funds have unique asset–liability profiles, they need highly idiosyncratic benchmarks. One fund might have a lot of current retirees. Its benchmark should reflect its need for steady cash flows in order to pay the monthly checks. Another fund might have hundreds of young members whose contributions will not be required to support retirement for several decades. This fund ought to have an entirely different benchmark. Yet both funds probably hire managers whose stated goal is to outperform the S&P 500 index.

In practice, most funds adopt the same benchmarks, regardless of whether they are sensible. They will not hesitate to sack a manager who underperforms a benchmark, even though the underperformance might have no impact on the fund's health because the benchmark was set too high. Many mutual fund investors who are seduced by total return performance measures, and therefore follow leading market indexes, will similarly switch out of a fund that "underperforms," even though they might be better off not paying a set of transaction fees. The fund management industry is largely structured around measures that

make little sense for the vast majority of participants. A better understanding of benchmarks would suggest a quite different structure!

Asleep at the Wheel

Another demonstration of how benchmarks are influenced by scenarios is
to imagine that you are a child in the 1920s and your father acquires your
family's first car—a Model-T Ford. You are then struck by a mysterious illness that puts you to sleep for 60 years. When you wake in the 1980s, the
only car you have ever known is that old Ford—it is your benchmark for
cars. When you step into a new car, you are astounded by the smoothness
of the ride, the stylish body, the amazing speed! Actually, you are driving
a Trabant, one of those ugly East German vehicles that briefly became
fashionable after the fall of the Berlin Wall, before proper taste reasserted
itself! But *any* modern car, even a two-stroke smoke-emitting blob such as
the Trabant, hugely outperforms your benchmark because decades of
technology and design have made your benchmark ridiculous.

What is the right response? Faced with changed circumstances like
these, the sensible course is to change the benchmark. Very quickly, you
would realize that a Trabant is at the extreme low end of modern cars,
and you would switch your attention accordingly. When circumstances
became different, we should not hesitate to change our benchmark.
Imagine if you won a lottery and suddenly had more money than you
could spend. Your interest might move from $25,000 cars to $80,000
cars in the blink of an eye and the growl of an Alfa Spider's engine.

The same approach holds true with, say, paintings and other art
forms. We set our benchmarks using a combination of aesthetic and
economic factors. Indeed, critics perform a social function in this respect. By arguing about what is great art or who is the best soprano,
critics compete to create benchmarks for future comparisons. When
we have a little money, we might buy an etching or a limited edition
print. Money is a large factor in defining our benchmark. If we set our

sights too high, we will never be satisfied with what we buy, or we might spend unaffordable amounts on pictures from an expensive gallery—the equivalent of taking too much risk in pursuit of an impossible rate of return. But if we became rich, money would play a sharply reduced role and we might unleash a passion for Rodin sculptures.

Again, although they might not know it consciously, companies and managers everywhere know instinctively that benchmarks are scenario-dependent. Take the fuss in 1997 over the proposed multibillion-dollar merger of BT and MCI, two giant telecom firms that joined in a desire to become a transatlantic monster. When it was announced in November 1996, the then $22 billion deal was heralded as the merger of two confident firms with two mostly satisfied sets of shareholders, albeit shareholders who felt both firms could do with a jolt of energy. Both managements saw great Upside from the deal. And both felt that competition in their industry was so intense that there would be big potential Regret if they did not merge. Alone, the two companies feared being too small to survive. These similar benchmarks led each firm to adopt a bold position, and a deal was struck.

The managers at BT made their offer for MCI using an established benchmark. They had no reason to doubt the scenario under which they were paying a full price for a fast-growing and successful firm. Indeed, they gave more weight to the nasty strategic consequences of not merging than they did to the danger of paying too much.

Unfortunately, things changed. While negotiations were under way, the fact emerged that MCI was not as healthy as its managers had maintained. Its earnings were likely to be far less than expected by BT. When this news hit the market, MCI shares fell sharply, which had the effect of making the previously announced merger price seem far too high.

Under this new scenario, BT had no choice but to alter its benchmark. It had to give a greater weight to the purchase price. It still wanted to merge with MCI, but it faced bigger Regret if it paid too much, not least because it could be sued by its own shareholders. Under some pressure, BT renegotiated terms with MCI's managers, extracting a 15 percent cut in the price. (Subsequently, this deal became even more complex. WorldCom later became a rival bidder for MCI, and drops in WorldCom share prices complicated negotiations. The would-be merger became a case study of how benchmarks need to be shifted in response to new circumstances, as well as a fine example of how scenarios should be changed to reflect changes in the environment.)

BT is not the only firm that knows how badly things can go wrong when we pick, or stick with, the wrong benchmarks. Most people have forgotten by now, but as recently as the early 1990s banks all around the world were in trouble. In America, it was feared that the entire financial system was on the brink of collapse. In Europe, leading institutions were humbled by huge losses as they wrote off loans they should never have made. Several large banks did collapse; others, notably Citicorp in America, Crédit Lyonnais in France, and Barclays in Britain, struggled to survive. It was easy enough to spot the symptoms of trouble—balance sheets were bloated as a result of a collective lending binge that placed the emphasis on growth rather than risk.

But what was the *cause?* Influenced by one another, banks were looking at the wrong benchmarks. They thought that growth of their lending business was good, regardless of who the borrowers were, and that only the biggest lenders would survive the industry's cutthroat competition. They measured themselves by two main benchmarks: (1) the general rate at which loans were growing, and (2) the specific rates at which rivals were growing. Loan officers found themselves under pressure to bring in new business at almost any cost. Meanwhile, other areas of banking were ignored or accorded secondary status. One foreign exchange trader recalls with bitterness how, in the early 1990s, his trading floor would be brought to a halt at least once daily. The traders, who were subjected to strict limits because of the supposed risks of their business, were required to applaud as a proud loan officer marched through the room bearing the latest loan agreement. The bank in question was Bank of New England. It went bust, thanks to the very loan officers whose performance was compulsorily applauded and who were often rewarded with outlandish bonuses simply for bringing in new business.

Spread across thousands of banks, the consequences of this behavior were awful. It was as if banks had forgotten the basic rules of their industry. Leading firms ended up with huge exposures to developers of office buildings. When the buildings could not find tenants, the borrowers could not pay their loans. Banks wrote off billions, all because they had adopted the wrong benchmark.

This example is useful because it is easy to see how choosing the wrong benchmark almost predetermined that bad decisions would follow. When they endorsed loan growth as their benchmark, managers of banks sent a powerful signal to their employees. Loan officers could see tremendous Upside from simply lending more money and could also see that they might suffer Regret if they were too persnickety toward new business. There were no rewards for *not* lending. From the perspective of banks' shareholders, this was akin to opening a cash faucet and throwing away the plug.

It should come as no surprise that, since their early 1990s debacle, many banks have adopted different benchmarks. Unfortunately, many of them have chosen the hurdle rate approach that we criticized earlier. But it is common practice now to measure loan officers not just by the business they bring in but also by the business they turn down. Risk has been factored into the equation.

Bad experiences have changed how other firms choose their benchmarks. Elizabeth Glaeser, a consultant with Deloitte & Touche in New York, tells the story of Texaco and Chevron, two oil firms. In theory, these companies should have similar benchmarks because their businesses are almost identical. In practice, however, there are some apparently baffling differences. Both must borrow huge sums to fund their ongoing operations and their search for new oil reserves. But whereas Texaco tries to borrow much of its money over long periods,

Chevron tries to keep all of its debt at the shortest possible maturity. At any given time, Chevron thus has an enormous portfolio of what is known as commercial paper—short-term bills that typically mature and must be repaid three months after they are issued. To fund itself, Chevron is constantly issuing new paper as existing debt matures. When money is plentiful, Chevron's funding costs are cheap, in part because it is not borrowing any one investor's money for very long. By contrast, Texaco has higher funding costs because it tries to lock in investors' cash for five, ten, or even thirty years.

Why would two similar firms adopt such different approaches to funding themselves? More to the point, can both be right? The answer to the first question lies in the firms' different choices of benchmarks. The key to understanding Texaco's behavior is that this firm went bankrupt in 1987 and was rescued by a costly $3 billion loan put together by a group of banks that stood to lose even more if Texaco went under altogether. As a result, Texaco's managers acquired firsthand experience of what can happen when a firm is unable to borrow new funds in the open market. The liquidity it normally relies on disappears when lenders think they might not get their money back—a concern that clearly applies in a bankruptcy. With this direct knowledge of Regret in mind, Texaco's benchmark for funding is set less aggressively than Chevron's, and it can justify paying more overall for its funds. Whether they are ignorant of or simply unconcerned by this liquidity risk, Chevron's managers have chosen a benchmark based on an assumption that the funding they require will always be available. Because they have not yet absorbed the lesson of Regret, they are content to chase short-term savings at the expense of greater flexibility in the event of future trouble.

Individuals also have to be careful about setting the right benchmark. Earlier, we mentioned how, in choosing a house, it is important to pick a benchmark that is appropriate for the market in which someone is buying. An index of Tokyo rentals is of no use if you are buying in New York. But even if we stick to this observation, we can go wrong because we might choose a local benchmark that guarantees we will suffer

Regret. Let's assume we are buying a house in London. It would be a big mistake to pick a $4 million mansion in Belgravia or New York's Gramercy Park as our benchmark. Most other houses would simply never measure up, so we would be miserable in whatever home we bought. If we decided to buy in more trendy Islington, it would be equally foolish to take the nicest house in that neighborhood as our benchmark. We need to adopt a more useful measure, so we imagine an "average" house and base our comparisons accordingly. Because "average" is a somewhat vacuous concept, house buying can be frustrating. It is quite difficult to compare a house with a basement to another that has a loft extension. Nevertheless, we do it, so strong is our need for benchmarks.

Perhaps the ultimate benchmark is the price of money. But this benchmark gives economists great trouble. For one thing, it is difficult to measure prices accurately, especially as they change over time. Measuring our material progress is particularly tricky. It might seem easy to measure the price of, say, a ballpoint pen. But suppose a new pen comes along that costs twice as much and lasts four times as long. If it catches on, the price paid for a pen has doubled but the price of using a pen has been halved. If we were trying to measure living standards or the real cost of living, the second price is the one that we should use. In practice, it can be extremely difficult to observe price changes of this kind. Think of the debate raging in developed economies about the impact of computers on labor productivity. It is a fine example of the confusion that can be caused as new services are introduced and then refined. How do we compare the communication services provided by a modern telephone with those of a 1950s model?

William Nordhaus, an economist at Yale University, explored these issues a few years ago. Looking for a service that had changed little, despite technological innovations, he lit upon a brilliant idea: Why not look at how much it has cost to illuminate the spaces we live in? After all, a Babylonian lamp was used for much the same purpose as a modern electric bulb. With great ingenuity, Nordhaus collected data on "light services" and their prices through the ages. Among the light sources he examined were: burning sticks; fat- and oil-burning lamps; candles (tallow, sperm oil, etc.); gaslights of various kinds; kerosene lamps; and the many different kinds of electric light. The unit of measurement for light is a lumen. A single wax candle emits about 13 lumens; a modern 100-watt light bulb on a 110-volt electrical line emits around 1,300 lumens.

The fascinating results show how easily we can be fooled by widely accepted benchmarks. In nominal terms, the price of 1,000 lumen hours has fallen from about 40 cents in 1800 to about one-tenth of one cent today. Bearing in mind that 40 cents in 1800 was equivalent to more than $4 in today's money, the results are even more startling.

Now compare these data to the official benchmarks. The conventional method of gathering statistics looks at the price of goods that provide light rather than at the price of the light itself. According to this measure, the nominal price of light has risen by 180 percent since 1800! In other words, this benchmark suggests that the price of light in 1800 was four-hundredths of one cent per 1,000 lumen hours—1,000 times cheaper than the price implied by Nordhaus's measure. The magnitude of the difference is mostly the result of compounding a small number over 200 years—the annual drift between the two series is less than 4 percent, but this becomes vast over time. We rely on conventional wisdom to our peril. Small wonder that defining the impact of new technologies on living standards and productivity causes so much trouble today.

Once we understand benchmarks better, as with other elements of our risk paradigm, we can begin to do some interesting things. Armed with correct knowledge, we can better decide how to choose our bases for comparison. We can use benchmarks to ask new questions about what we are trying to measure, or what we should be trying to measure. Central banks that seek price stability generally use price inflation as their benchmark for setting interest rates. But what if they are measuring the wrong things? The components that make up the benchmark need careful assembly.

How Banks Use Benchmarks

We can also use the idea of benchmarks to shed light on real risk management problems that firms face every day. In Chapter 4, we introduced the idea of Value at Risk (VaR). We were not altogether flattering about it, mostly because we think that, by itself, it gives an inadequate view of risk. But we cannot deny that VaR has to be taken seriously. Since it was popularized by J. P. Morgan in 1994, with the release of its RiskMetrics software and data, VaR has been broadly sanctioned by regulators as a way for financial institutions to measure "market risk" — the risk attached to price changes in the instruments they hold at any given moment.

We think that VaR can be greatly improved by using benchmarks better. To see this, let's step into the arcane world of finance once more. In an ideal world, a market risk measure should:

- Capture the risk exposure of trading books (these are, in effect, ledgers in which individual deals are aggregated) when a significant shift in the market occurs.

- Determine the efficiency of these books; i.e., could the risk in the book be reduced without affecting returns?

- Account for the differences among markets, such as the underlying market volatility, the cost of capital, the liquidity risk, and so on.

- Compare risk across different markets.

- Assist firms in their capital allocation decisions.

All of these characteristics seem straightforward enough; we wouldn't need advanced degrees in finance to make such a list from scratch. But does VaR meet these tests? Can it be used to compare trading books across markets? Is it at all useful as a guide to decisions on how we might allocate our capital to different trading books? Can it be a source of useful input for strategic planning?

Answers to these questions depend on the intended use of VaR in the institution. If it is purely to measure market risk—that is, to understand the possible amount a portfolio could lose or gain over some period—then we would give VaR a qualified endorsement. However, we think that some of the methodologies that have been proposed for computing VaR could be poor predictors of a trading book's actual behavior. And when it comes to strategic risk management purposes, such as comparing trading desks and capital allocation, then we think VaR is inadequate.

There are three main drawbacks to VaR from a strategic perspective:

1. The measure does not permit meaningful comparisons across markets. It therefore fails to meet a basic requirement for a meaningful measure.
2. It does not give any information on the risk/reward trade-off in a given market and therefore cannot provide useful input to the capital allocation process. It gives us no clear idea as to the best place to put our money.
3. VaR is potentially misleading for portfolios that contain lots of derivatives with complex payoffs.

To illustrate the first drawback, imagine a bank that has two trading desks, one for New Zealand equities and the other for U.S. Treasury bonds. Assume that both have a VaR of $10 million. What may we infer from this number? Are they both equally risky? Would we allocate the same amount of capital to both?

They are certainly not equally risky. For one thing, liquidity in these two markets is vastly different. The cost of capital in each market is likely to be very different. Moreover, in some future period, our current estimates (which we would use to compute scenarios) of possible future values for liquidity and cost of capital would most likely be different again in the two markets. This will be true for almost any measure that could have an effect on the exposure of the two desks—yields, volatility, assumptions about correlations, and so on. The absolute levels of all market risk parameters will differ, but, more importantly, the volatility of these parameters will differ greatly.

Asset managers deal with this problem by measuring performance across markets via benchmarks that reflect the peculiarities of each market. By measuring relative to a benchmark (usually a market index), one measures only the gains or losses of an investment that is "average" for that market.

Some banks argue that benchmarking is not relevant for traders. From the perspective of risk management and the allocation of trading capital, however, benchmarking is eminently relevant. In the above example, for each of the two markets (New Zealand equities and U.S. Treasury bonds), there is an (almost) riskless trade that will yield a small but positive return (differing for the two markets). The riskless trade is often a good benchmark. If our traders do some other trade, we can posit that they are choosing it over the riskless trade. Importantly, the alternative trade will yield an expected return whose value will typically depend on the market scenarios that are likely over the chosen time horizon. We refer to the riskless trade as the benchmark or target portfolio.

In financial trading, as in everything else, there are many possible benchmarks. The choice is a function of the institution's appetite for risk. Choosing a benchmark with a very high return will force traders to adopt risky strategies. Ideally, the benchmark should be a good proxy for the market, an "average" trade that can be executed easily. In the equity market, we would choose an appropriate equity index. In the U.S. Treasury market, we might use a three-month T-Bill.

Remember, too, how important it is for benchmarks to be scenario-dependent. A natural benchmark in New Zealand will possibly be more volatile than the corresponding benchmark in the United States.

Alternatively stated, the New Zealand benchmark has a VaR that is greater than the VaR of the corresponding benchmark in the United States. It follows that the logical way to compare traders across disparate markets is to measure their exposure relative to the benchmark. Without that measure, a trader holding a portfolio in New Zealand equities might have a VaR that is the same as that of a trader holding a U.S. Treasury portfolio. Yet the New Zealand trader might be exhibiting very poor performance in his market whereas the U.S. Treasury trader could be performing very well in hers.

We need to calculate VaR relative to the appropriate benchmarks and not in the absolute. Instead of simple VaR, we need to measure how much the portfolio varies around a predetermined benchmark. We call this the Benchmark-Value-at-Risk or B-VaR. Formally, B-VaR is defined as the Value-at-Risk of a portfolio consisting of a long position in the original portfolio plus a short position in the benchmark portfolio. B-VaR is not calculated as the difference between the VaR of the portfolio and the VaR of the benchmark!

Naturally, the choice of benchmark is subjective and context-dependent. For most markets and for most banks, however, natural benchmarks exist. For example, these could be market indexes, carefully selected portfolios, hurdle rates set as strategic objectives and then reset as circumstances alter, or interest rates such as Libor (the rate at which banks lend to each other), with or without spreads added.

This "language of benchmarks" in finance might seem a little complicated. The important thing to bear in mind is that it helps enormously, in all kinds of decisions, to identify an appropriate benchmark. And, as with scenarios, it can make a big difference if we know that we are using a benchmark. We have already shown a couple of examples where understanding that the wrong benchmark was at work threw new light on old problems. Other examples can show how pervasive benchmarks really are.

Take the thorny and hotly debated question of whether firms should hedge some of their risks, using derivatives to lay off exposures. Some argue that managers should always use hedging to get rid of risks they either do not understand or feel uncomfortable with. Others argue that, in the context of an investor's overall portfolio, there are always natural hedges, and a single firm's managers should simply concentrate on running their business. The debate about hedging is usually juxtaposed with the idea of diversification: if you can't hedge a risk away, then you might be able to reduce it by diversifying into some other uncorrelated risk. Many of the risks that firms can hedge are price risks; exposure to oil and other commodity prices is a good example. Exposure to fluctuations in foreign currencies is another. These are "systematic" risks, and, say fans of hedging, it is perfectly sensible for managers to do away with or minimize them.

The hedging problem can be helpfully described as a benchmarking issue. Let's look at the case of Merck, a drug company famous for having been a pioneer of foreign exchange hedging. Based in America, land of the dollar, Merck has 70-odd overseas subsidiaries producing lots of revenues in local currencies. But in the 1980s, as the dollar swung up and down, so did the value of Merck's non-American profits. This was a serious problem for Merck's top managers. After a review, they decided that it was imperative to hedge their exposure to exchange rate fluctuations. Objectors asked: Why? After all, on the face of it, this meant paying significant amounts in transaction and other costs, and it was open to debate whether there was a tangible economic benefit to the firm. The managers were adamant, however, for a single overwhelming reason. They could not live with the risk that, in a given year, they might lose money in dollars because of exchange rates, to the extent that the firm's efforts in research and development could be compromised. That was territory into which they simply did not wish to travel.

For those Merck managers, the possible interruption of research and development (R&D) was intolerable—their business depends on new products for continued growth. They embraced the dollar level of income necessary to sustain the R&D program as a benchmark. They might take more (or less) risk in hedging their foreign income streams, but the baseline was the integrity of R&D funding. Viewed in this way, the decision for Merck to hedge makes perfect sense. Regardless of other considerations, shareholders simply could not argue with the implications of the chosen benchmark.

We can add other elements of our risk framework and enrich this picture further. The intolerable risk was an expression of the Merck managers' potential Regret—their risk-adjusted calculation with respect to foreign exchange led them to place great weight on the downside. They used hedging to insure themselves against the risk, up to the point where R&D funding would be secure. Thereafter, they were as happy to self-insure as the next firm. But their chosen benchmark mandated a particular level of hedging because they could not live with the Regret of anything less.

Let's now test this strategy in other firms. Think of any kind of constraint that managers have placed on a firm. It might be: No more than 10 percent of sales to one customer or in one market. Or perhaps: After a certain level of exposure, a price risk must be hedged. Each of these constraints is, in effect, a benchmark for risk—and each is an expression of the firm's attitude toward Regret. One international fund management firm has a brilliant and mysterious computer model that tries to act as if it were a real person with knowledge of markets and how they work. The model adores risk. If it thinks it is right about something, it is prepared to go all out in pursuit of high returns. But real customers cannot live with the Regret of big losses if the model gets it wrong. So the fund managers added constraints: for instance, the model cannot place 90 percent of its money in a single country. Constraints like this form the benchmarks against which models should be measured. From fund managers' perspective, it is vital that clients understand those benchmarks. Otherwise, there might be major misunderstandings.

When investors are told about and understand any constraints adopted by a firm's managers, there cannot be much useful argument about whether hedging is appropriate. The key is disclosure. If every firm listed its benchmarks, then investors could take these into account when allocating their money. Perhaps, in the future, firms will be required by accounting rules to spell out the benchmarks they are using. They will then minimize the risk that they might mislead investors as to the nature of their businesses.

Think how much better off investors would be if they knew both the benchmarks and the scenarios that were being adopted by firms in which they own shares. Today, we find out only after the event that things have gone wrong—often months later, when annual reports are compiled. In the future, we might take for granted that we know the "bets" our managers are taking and the extent to which they are "insured" against the downside. This knowledge would give us a much better basis on which to make forward-looking decisions. And, strangely, this communication might help managers because they can make explicit the benchmarks against which they wish to be compared.

Benchmarks can be a powerful tool for understanding how people and firms behave. They add to our understanding of how we make contracts with other people. Two parties with different benchmarks can rationally reach a deal because the benchmarks inform their risk-adjusted calculations and allow them to place different values on the same price. Benchmarks explain why two firms that, in theory, should act identically may, in practice, take opposite tacks. With implied views, they add a powerful weapon to the negotiator's arsenal. If you can figure out your opponent's benchmark, you are at least halfway to figuring out how to make your offer look attractive. Finally, benchmarks suggest ways in which firms might rethink how they set performance goals and how they communicate their rationale to investors. Who would have thought that the goal of keeping up with the Joneses could hide such a rich panoply of ideas?

Chapter 6

PAYING FOR PLAYING

It is important to understand that a risk aversion constant such as lambda is not some obscure measure that is useful only for financial calculations. It also works as a way of explaining all kinds of decisions we make as consumers. When we buy insurance, for instance, we are expressing our aversion to risk. But what seems at first a simple transaction can hide complex and subtle information about our view of risk.

Consumers shopping for auto insurance, for example, face a range of choices. At one extreme, they can opt for the minimum coverage (cheap) required by law; at the other, they can purchase a comprehensive policy (very expensive) that covers them for every potential outcome. Few consumers, unless economically constrained, actually pick one of the extremes, however. Most people choose a position somewhere in between—a level of coverage with which they feel comfortable. Many pay a lower premium by accepting a deductible: if they make a claim, they must pay the first $200, say, before they receive money from the insurer. Careful drivers who think they are likely to have few claims will feel comfortable with a larger deductible than someone with poor peripheral vision who regularly has small scrapes. Indeed, that person might not want any deductible at all, although the policy will be correspondingly more costly.

How can we explain why most people choose not to buy full coverage? Affordability provides part of the answer. People with very little money often buy the minimum insurance required by law—they cannot afford to spend more. But they also have very little to lose, so they will behave accordingly, taking minimum coverage to protect only against disaster. We all have our own Regret threshold, which determines the ratio we set between self-insurance and actual insurance. The simple answer is: protection against every eventuality is very expensive, and most of us want only protection against the worst outcome—a crash or incident that could lead to bankruptcy. We trade off coverage against lesser disasters because the cost of insuring gets progressively higher, the more outcomes we try to cover.

So, we accept a $200 deductible because we know that paying even several penalties will not break us financially. But we cannot accept a multimillion-dollar risk that would destroy our lives if it came to pass. In effect, we are assigning to risk a value that determines how much coverage we feel we need to buy.

Intuitively, we know that the chances of being in a catastrophic crash that wrecks the car and causes a fatality are very small. To insure against that outcome ought to be very cheap because the occurrence is rare and the insurer will reap many premiums before it has to pay out. So why are we willing to pay $1,000 annually for coverage that ought to cost 50 cents? The reason is that we cannot contemplate that horrendous outcome, so we set an extremely high value on insurance against it. We will (and millions of consumers regularly do) pay way over the odds to protect against that unacceptable exposure. Insurers understand Regret!

Regarding our $200 deductible, we know that we have already covered the worst outcomes when the insurer offers us what is actually a bet. In effect, we have reduced our potential Regret to a level we can cope with. For a lower up-front payment, we can now assume some of the risk attached to bad, but not disastrous, outcomes. The insurer is sharing the risk with us, in return for a share of the premium. So why accept a deductible? If we have a few minor scrapes and bumps, we feel sanguine about paying for the first part of the damage because the bills won't make us bankrupt. In this calculation, we are much less risk averse; in effect, we set a lower value on risk in judging our insurance needs at this level.

There are endless possible variations on this analysis. We may feel differently about a $500 deductible, for example. And when we insure the lives of our family, rather than our cars, we take positions that relate our expectations of risk to our ability to survive financially in the event of a death in the family. When we buy home insurance, we weigh the risk of a flood or a fire against our ability to start again should the unthinkable occur. When huge natural catastrophes occur—such as the floods that devastated America's northern midwest region in 1997—we look to government agencies to bear some of the costs of the downside. When Regret is widespread, affected businesses and individuals don't mind calling on the government for millions of dollars' worth of help.

Regret also throws interesting light on an enduring mystery. Many fewer people buy disability insurance than ought to—after all, the odds of a disabling accident or illness affecting us are high enough that most people whose work supports a family should insure against the possibility. Such insurance appears to be expensive. But if people thought about the Regret they would experience if they found that they were not only physically disabled but also financially ruined, they might think harder about disability insurance. They ought in this case to assign a high value to Regret and be prepared to pay significant premiums for peace of mind. Another reason is more speculative: people do not like to think about mortality or disability, even though one is inevitable and the other is possible. Young people, who face the biggest Regret from disability because they might live for many years, are understandably reluctant to ponder their own incapacity or demise. The absence of an obvious Upside in scenarios that involve disability probably contributes to this widespread reluctance!

Another aspect of some young people's behavior can be explained in the same way. Think of how drugs are developed and tested by pharmaceutical firms. Would you swallow a pill that might make you ill, in return for $100? Probably you would not. But college students often volunteer to be guinea pigs; in return for modest cash payments, they take doses of as-yet-unlicensed drugs. If they suffer side effects over the course of the tests, the manufacturer goes back to the laboratory and refines the formula. A middle-aged person with children would never dream of taking a substance with unknown effects, in return for a few hundred dollars. Yet thousands of young people will do this. Why? They weight the immediate Upside of cash far more than any Regret from possible side effects of the drugs. Because they have relatively few responsibilities, but often have difficulty financing themselves through college, acting as a guinea pig seems like a good idea. The "work" is less demanding and better paid than flipping burgers or waiting on tables, and seems like a good risk-adjusted deal.

Arguably, when they take this risk, they are placing too low a value on Regret. We can show this by simply rephrasing our original question: In return for $100, would you take a pill that in an earlier trial caused 1 in 1,000 people permanently to lose the use of their left leg? Using our risk management framework, the students should ask how much it would cost to insure their left legs. The amount would almost certainly be more than $100, so this deal suddenly makes no sense at all. On a risk-adjusted basis, far fewer people would volunteer for testing.

In general, if we think an event has a very low probability but its consequences could be very painful, then we should seek to insure against it. Losing a leg would be catastrophic, so we would seek other ways of making $100.

We should always be prepared to contemplate extreme scenarios. Let's assume that we give them very small probabilities. In the unlikely event that a nasty thing happens, provided our Regret is fairly small, the net effect on our risk-adjusted value will also be small; including some extreme outcome won't change the deal much. But if the Regret seems big, then the net effect on our risk-adjusted value is substantial; indeed, the extreme scenarios can help us to identify where our Regret might come from.

It would be wrong to stop students and others from acting as guinea pigs if they still choose to do so. At some level, it is in society's best interest to know that drugs have been thoroughly tested before they are released for general sale. But if people were asked the question in a way that made them more aware of their potential downside, then the use of Regret analysis might significantly raise the price of human testing. Drug companies would think this a very bad thing—their profits would fall. But it might be a step toward solving the problem of student debt!

The balancing of Upside (in the form of better treatments and survival rates) and Regret (in the form of side effects or exacerbation of other conditions) neatly explains how many medical decisions are made. Where an illness is seen as particularly scary or threatening, society and individuals tend to assign a low lambda to medical decisions; greater risks are tolerated in the pursuit of an effective treatment. Drug treatments for AIDS and cancer frequently are expensive both financially and medically. Many AIDS patients take a costly cocktail of drugs that would harm a healthy person. The radiotherapy and drugs used to treat cancer often kill or damage healthy surrounding tissue as they seek out unhealthy parts. We accept that people undergoing chemotherapy will often lose their hair and suffer from debilitating illness in addition to their underlying condition. But the Upside—a cure or remission—is seen as worth the Regret of the short-term suffering.

People who suffer from serious conditions often have a very small chance of survival. As a nasty cancer progresses, for instance, doctors might calculate that a patient has a 1 in 10,000 chance of surviving. This represents a tiny chance at the ultimate Upside. But most doctors will still recommend treatment—for fear of lawsuits, or because they believe the patient has sufficient reserves to face the downside of further medication. But a patient with an advanced cancer sometimes makes a calculation that is different from the doctors'. If there is only a very slim chance or no chance of a cure, it can be better for an exhausted patient to forgo treatment and incur less net suffering. This is often the decision of patients who have endured previous unsuccessful treatments and simply cannot face another round.

Medicine can cast cases of great complexity. Indeed, although they rarely do it consciously, doctors are great users of scenarios and have a keen sense of the downside. It is standard practice to brief patients on the possible courses a condition might take and the risks attached to each course. Facing a complicated multiple-birth pregnancy, for instance, the parents might be told that one of the fetuses has an untreatable condition and its continued growth could threaten the viability of the other fetuses. Doctors might then present several possible courses of action: do nothing, try to stop the sick fetus from growing, or terminate the entire pregnancy and try again. Most couples would find these choices bewildering—and not just because deep moral issues are involved. Without a risk framework, it is impossible to make a considered choice between such alternatives.

Why do some couples opt for amniocentesis, a procedure that violates many of the ordinary rules of medicine? Normally, doctors would go to some lengths to avoid interfering with a developing fetus and its protective sac. An amnio test involves putting a needle into the pregnant women's abdomen and drawing off several vials of amniotic fluid, all the while trying not to prick the adjacent baby. Even in ideal circumstances, the procedure carries a small risk of spontaneous miscarriage. Moreover, couples who accept the procedure do so in the almost certain knowledge that if it reveals a fetus that has a chromosomal disorder such as Down's syndrome, they will terminate the pregnancy. After all, there is little point in undergoing the procedure if there is no intent to act on the knowledge gained.

On the face of it, this is a strange set of decisions. But Regret provides an explanation. People undergo the test because they cannot accept the Regret of being responsible for a handicapped child. Adverse test results pose a very difficult decision. Indeed, some controversial debates have occurred on this subject. In Britain, for example, the son of a former finance minister made a public fuss a few years ago when his wife bore a daughter with Down's syndrome. In a newspaper article, he argued that the existence of such a lovely child was by itself sufficient evidence that abortion should be outlawed. His high moral tone led to a flood of counterarguments. But a simple observation might have focused the debate in a different direction. He and his family were rich. Although they suffered the same emotional Regret as any other family that produces a handicapped child, they were well equipped financially to care for their daughter. This base confidence is not widespread. Most people shudder when they contemplate the financial burden of providing proper care and schooling for a sick child. It is simply beyond their means and, again, is an area where government help is often required. This is not to say that they are incapable of loving a sick child. But when they weigh the risks of handicap, most people must consider money as well as morals. Even though they might find an abortion morally devastating, their Regret is such that they cannot consider otherwise. A sensitive risk-adjusted analysis of such matters leads to two conclusions: (1) morals cannot be the only consideration in medical decisions; and (2) people's unique Regret factors define this as an area where governments meddle at their peril.

In a litigious society, doctors order more tests than are required because their Regret can be enormous if they don't—they might be sued by a patient. But where do they draw the line? Why don't they order every feasible test? Why do they stop at a few? The reason is that they make an Upside–Regret calculation. By doing a few tests, doctors reduce the Regret to a manageable level—they reduce the risk of being sued. But they also keep the Upside; by not ordering every possible test for every single patient, they are less likely to be dropped by their medical insurers.

It may seem obvious, but the reason why health insurance is such a politically charged issue in the United States and elsewhere is because the costs (Regret) to families and individuals of serious illness or conditions requiring long-term care are so disastrous that they are equivalent to ruin. Anyone who has been sick (or pregnant) in the United States, for instance, knows the lurch of fear that accompanies bad news from a doctor. Along with the medical shock comes the immediate worry: Can I afford the treatment? People without medical insurance often go without care because they cannot pay for treatment or even for a simple prescription. Those who are notionally covered know that there are always circumstances in which they might face enormous bills. A 20 percent share of $10,000, say, is beyond most families' means. Unusually, health represents a case where our Upside is measured not purely in dollars (although sometimes the ability to resume work must be put this way), but in relief that we will recover or feel better. We all want health insurance because our potential Regret almost always outweighs that relief. Interestingly, however, people who have suffered from an illness, or who have immediate experience of illness, will attach a higher lambda to their desire for insurance than those who have not been ill.

More people are facing serious Regret due to the move in several countries toward the privatization of care for the elderly. Families are learning that, to place Granny in a nice old folks' home, they have to lay out very large cash amounts. Granny herself may have accumulated sufficient assets to cover her care for a few years, but families are increasingly facing unexpected financial burdens at a stage when they are already overextended. And not all old people are financially responsible. Some can be profligate spenders even though they have very limited incomes.

These circumstances can cause serious Regret. Even as they plan financially for their own retirements, many families are finding that they need to put money aside in case they have to fund an aging relative. Or, they must anticipate when Granny's money will run out and the cash drain will be transferred to them. This unfortunate and unhappy situation can cause loved ones who deserve care and respect to be less and less tolerated as their assets dwindle. The stress on these families can be enormous. Because many developed countries have aging populations, the care of the elderly might become a much higher-profile political issue as more and more ordinary families become exposed to the Regret of insufficient funds.

There are plenty of parallels to retail auto and health insurance in the world of professional banking. Imagine a bank that has a $1 billion trading position in Russian shares. It fears that a market collapse in the next month might wipe out the entire position, an outcome that would force it into bankruptcy. For this bank, lambda has a very high value. Interestingly, in financial markets, a bank can often buy protection against the losses that would wipe it out. It can reduce its risk of losses to manageable levels.

The underlying point is that Regret and risk-adjusted values usefully model how we feel and behave in real situations. They remind us of the basic rules of risk management stated at the beginning of this book. We think about future outcomes that might affect us adversely, and our specific circumstances shape our appetite for risk. As we look forward, what feels fine one day feels intolerable the next.

Judging Regret

There are many other applications of risk-adjusted value and Regret. People often face an agonizing decision at some point in their business or personal lives: Should they go to court to contest a point of law? Filing a lawsuit, or defending against one, is a risk-laden business. The costs (Regret) of losing can be enormous. Sometimes these costs are financial; corporations such as Dow Corning have had heavy damages awarded against them. On other occasions, the costs can be less tangible but are nevertheless of great importance to the parties. In a libel case, for example, where one side is defending its good name, the outcome can have both financial and reputational Regret at stake! Lawsuits often involve tremendous potential Upside, too. Imagine you were suing for patent infringement on a best-selling drug you had invented. You might stand to gain millions in restitution. Or imagine you were suing for compensation for an injury. Again, millions are often at stake.

Let's look at Dow Corning in more detail. When a firm sets out to make a device such as a breast implant, the worst case it faces is that people might die because of the device. This is a serious possibility whenever a firm is dealing with a mass market. If things go wrong, the ensuing lawsuits could drive the firm out of business. In that case, it might make sense to research the device further and delay its sale. Dow Corning faced an extreme scenario that carried really big Regret. And there was a reasonable chance that the adverse event could happen. Firms can lower the probability of ruinous lawsuits by taking more time to test their products and by reducing the downside to the point where the product actually pays offs. But sometimes the lure of immediate Upside in the form of faster profits proves a fatal distraction.

In America, lawyers have found a way of simplifying how lawsuits are evaluated by potential litigants. For instance, many lawyers work on a contingency-fee basis. The would-be litigant pays nothing if he or she loses, but gives the lawyers a big percentage of any award. In effect, the lawyers have insured the plaintiffs' downside by writing an expensive premium on their potential Upside. People who might otherwise feel that a suit would be too expensive can now rationalize initiating an action because if they lose they have only minimal Regret. If they win, it might dawn on them that their lawyer has done rather well by way of compensation. But provided that does not reduce their award to a meaningless amount, then most people will accept this cost. Although the transaction is rarely characterized as such, when a plaintiff signs up a lawyer on a contingency fee, the lawyer is given a call option on some of the plaintiff's potential Upside! Thus, have derivatives played their part in encouraging America's legendary litigiousness?

There is an exact parallel to legal contingency fees in investment banking. Known as "range forwards," these derivative instruments are call options in which the buyer pays nothing up front but gives up some of the potential Upside instead.

Our concepts of Upside and Regret, seen through the prism of lambda, allow us to evaluate legal decisions from an interesting new perspective. It frustrates legal experts that big cases that involve major and interesting points of law are very often settled out of court. The points of law then remain vague because there is no judgment. But why are so many cases of this nature settled out of court, particularly where the battling businesses are answerable to shareholders?

Bankers Trust is a leading investment bank and one of America's biggest banks. Based in New York, but with offices around the world, it has long prided itself on fostering and rewarding a culture of innovation. Indeed, under Charles Sanford, its chairman and chief executive during the 1980s and early 1990s, Bankers Trust was at the crest of a wave of invention that swept across financial markets. It acquired a deserved reputation for being smarter and faster than rivals at finding and applying ways of managing financial risks of all kinds. To do this, it embraced two main ideas:

1. Derivatives were the key to unlocking a new era in which risks could be bundled and unbundled in any way that suited a particular transaction. Firms and investors could literally decide how much risk they wished to take and how much they wanted to lay off.

2. This technology was so powerful that no big corporation could afford to ignore it—which implied that the traditional close relationships between firms and old-fashioned banks were bound to break down. The rewards would go to the fastest and most innovative risk managers.

At the apogee of Bankers Trust's success in 1993, Sanford could proudly announce more than $1 billion of annual profits and some of the highest returns in the banking industry. Then things went horribly wrong. The problems faced by the bank have been written about extensively. For our purposes, the basic details will do. Several of the bank's customers, among them some well-known corporations, were badly burned by transactions that involved complicated and risky bets on movements in interest rates. In retrospect, some of these transactions were bizarre. For very small gains, firms were willing to place huge bets that had painful downside costs when they went wrong. One deal shaved a tiny fraction off the amount it cost a firm to borrow money, but the transaction exposed the firm to large losses if interest rates broke out of their recent pattern.

Why did respected (and respectable) firms embark on such crazy deals? A simple $U - R$ analysis would have told them that they should never have contemplated such large exposures for such miniscule returns. Add lambda into the calculation, and only the most gung-ho risk-seeking firms would ever have signed up for the deals that got Bankers Trust into trouble. And one wonders what shareholders might have said, had they known that their supposedly transparent and already risky investment was actually hiding far bigger risks that had nothing to do with the firm's reason for existing and their reason for investing? Put another way, if you invest in a leveraged hedge fund, you presumably expect your fund manager to take on all kinds of financial risk. If you buy shares in a tractor manufacturer, you don't expect it to be trading in exotic derivative contracts. If you find out that it is trading that way, you might well run for the nearest stock liquidation desk.

One explanation for such crazy behavior is that many firms at the time were recklessly chasing a chimera. They believed that they could encourage their own staff to improve the firm's financial performance by borrowing money ever more cheaply. The office of the treasurer, which is responsible for the money coming into and flowing out of a firm's coffers, was often given its own profit incentive. Treasurers were exhorted to lower the firm's overall cost of funds by playing clever, and sometime sensible enough, games. Personal rewards in the form of bonuses were usually given to those who could show that they had "made money" for the firm. Not surprisingly, many treasurers cared more about rewards than risk. They were predisposed to ignore or downplay Regret because, institutionally, they had clearly defined incentives. They certainly had limited Regret compared with the Regret faced by their corporation! By trying to create better performance, many managers actually exposed their shareholders to significant financial risks.

Nowhere was this more evident than at Procter & Gamble (P&G), a firm that is a worldbeater when it comes to diapers, soap powders, and dishwashing liquids but proved itself an ass at financial engineering. P&G had become an aggressive exponent of "profit-centered Treasury management," as well as a regular client of Bankers Trust and other big investment banks, notably J. P. Morgan. In 1994, however, it ran into an embarrassing problem. Some of its deals soured when interest rates unexpectedly began rising as part of the Federal Reserve Bank's effort to dampen the economy. Over the course of the year, the Fed progressively raised rates in a series of small increments. For P&G, the damage was done by the first couple of increases. Like Robert Citron, Orange County's hapless treasurer, P&G assumed a single-scenario forecast when it entered many of its deals: rates would not rise. Because of the highly leveraged structure of several of its "money-saving" deals, P&G had begun to rack up painful losses when the scenario was exposed in all its foolishness. By April, the firm cried foul. Nursing $195 million in losses, P&G refused to pay, alleging that Bankers Trust had misled its staff into buying inappropriate instruments. In October, it sued the bank, claiming that it should not have to pay up its losses, and requesting damages.

The case promised judgment on some fascinating issues. Bankers Trust was in an extremely unusual position. It had to defend itself against a customer that had not paid its bills and was using the courts as a way of exacting revenge for deals gone bad. If a leading bank could not rely on a leading corporation to honor its debts—and worse still, found itself in court defending its very reputation against serious charges—what future awaited American capitalism? The bank could show that P&G had entered willingly into the troublesome deals. Indeed, P&G had done similar deals with other banks and was considered a sophisticated counterparty. Moreover, P&G had spurned the chance to close off its exposures while its losses were still relatively small. Its stubbornness and its insistence on continuing its outrageous gambles were to blame for the extent of its losses.

P&G, on the other hand, had to explain its conduct to its shareholders. Why on earth was a consumer goods firm engaging in dangerous financial speculations? Answer: We didn't know how risky these deals were because dishonest bankers led us up the garden path. The firm ungraciously sacked its treasurer (its chairman later went, too). It became amply clear that its senior managers, including the chairman, had little idea of the scale of the treasurer's risk taking—a further embarrassment for a supposedly well-run firm. During its litigation against Bankers Trust, P&G was thus in the rare position of being managed by people who made a virtue out of not knowing what they were doing! P&G's adoption of an aggressive legal stance was perhaps not so surprising. Attack was the best form of defense.

Both sides, then, had very strong interests riding on their legal battle. Fundamental issues of principle were at stake. Lawyers were rubbing their hands in anticipation of fascinating and groundbreaking rulings from the trial judge.

There was no trial. Bankers Trust and P&G settled their case out of court in May 1996, less than a week before the trial was due to begin. Why? Let's look at the case from the perspective of each party.

By 1996, Bankers Trust had suffered enormous harm. It had sacked a couple of staff members and reassigned some others, and it had settled several other lawsuits—acts that implicitly admitted that something had been wrong in its sales culture. During pretrial proceedings, it had been hugely embarrassed when leaked tapes suggested that some of its sales staff had almost enjoyed misleading the bank's customers about the scale of their losses. These tapes gave the impression that some of the staff saw themselves in competition with less-than-bright customers and cared little if they came to harm. Battered, Sanford had retired as chairman and was replaced by Frank Newman, an outsider whose role was clearly to restore Bankers Trust's sullied name.

What was Bankers Trust's Upside in the legal battle with P&G? It could win the case, in which event it would stand to collect its $195 million debt from P&G, less some rather hefty legal fees. That was no small sum, but it represented a fraction of the amount needed for the bank to return to its glory days. Winning would perhaps have handed the bank some less tangible upside by allowing it to claim that it had been falsely accused by P&G and had not deserved all of the reputational damage it had suffered. Moreover, it would have become difficult for anyone else who had signed a contract to sue the bank. The precedent of a victory for Bankers Trust would have placed the onus on the bank's counterparties to understand and to be responsible for the risks they assumed in dealing with the bank. (One of P&G's legal strategies was to argue that the disastrous deals had never in fact been proper contracts and should therefore be declared invalid.)

But what of the bank's downside? It had already suffered costly damage. If it lost the case, it faced an unknown situation. It would certainly never collect the $195 million it was owed. P&G was also seeking punitive damages and had cited America's tough racketeering laws—an aggressive move that, in theory, could triple any damages awarded against the bank. The trial was to be held on P&G's home ground, exposing Bankers Trust to the risk that a sympathetic local jury might find for the "home team." Losing the case could also be the final straw for some of the bank's big investors, several of whom were already impatient for better performance. If they sold, the bank's share price would tumble.

Whichever way it viewed the various scenarios, Bankers Trust should have had an overwhelming desire to settle this case. Its potential Regret was far greater than its Upside. But add lambda into the picture. Under Sanford, the bank had embraced modern risk management techniques. When P&G sued, Sanford's instincts were to fight back in order to protect his bank's and his own reputation. He believed wholeheartedly in his bank's virtue, as well as in the vision of finance that Bankers Trust had aggressively espoused. He wanted to make the point that a contract is a contract, and he was prepared to risk further damage in pursuit of what he saw as natural justice. But where he thought the bank had acted wrongly, he moved quickly to settle lawsuits—as he had done in several cases in 1995.

This was not an entirely unreasonable position. Sanford's central assumption was that Bankers Trust had suffered its worst damage in the months after P&G filed the lawsuit. Losing the case would be bad, but not too bad when measured against the potential Upside were the bank to win. That turned out to be an incorrect judgment. The bank suffered more and horrible damage when incriminating tapes relating to another client were leaked in 1995. And the long-drawn-out fight with P&G kept the bank in the harsh glare of publicity far longer than would have been the case if it had simply settled and carried on with business. Firms that find themselves in this unfortunate position can struggle to escape, and the effect on morale and momentum is sapping.

From P&G's perspective, the case had significant Upside. If P&G won, it stood to walk away from $195 million of losses. It could also expect millions more in damages. Its downside was $195 million plus a few more millions in legal fees. Moreover, it might suffer reputational harm if its "We were dumb" defense strategy failed. It is one thing to claim you were ignorant, but quite another to have a court find that you were reckless as well as stupid! In general, however, it is easy to see why P&G was disinclined to settle with Bankers Trust, or at least why it played hardball in the few meetings that were held to discuss possible settlements. For instance, P&G was determined not to settle for less than had been awarded to another firm that had squared its differences with Bankers Trust. But P&G was determined, if possible, not to pay a cent to the bank.

In the weeks before the eventual settlement with P&G, Bankers Trust won a series of key rulings in pretrial debate. These rulings gave it more confidence even as they altered P&G's stance. For one thing, the trial judge appeared to limit the scope of the bank's downside. He suggested that because P&G had wilfully carried on with its disastrous bets, even after the bank had warned it that it was losing pots of money, it could not fairly blame Bankers Trust for all of its losses. In effect, Bankers Trust had made the bed, but P&G had turned down the sheets. The judge also wondered why P&G should be entitled to punitive damages when it had never paid up on its losses. In blunt fashion, he told P&G's lawyers, "The unique aspect of this case is that you haven't paid a red cent."

P&G suddenly faced a different situation. Its legal strategy had assumed that there would be significant Upside. Now the judge had capped that Upside and had potentially increased P&G's Regret by making it responsible for some of its losses. Small wonder that, in the final days before the trial was due to start, P&G came to terms with Bankers Trust. The risk-adjusted calculation for both sides was quite clear: there was too much downside for insufficient Upside. It was now in both parties' interests to settle, and a deal was duly struck.

Now for the Bad News

Upside, Regret, and lambda also offer an explanation for why firms sometimes cover up bad news that, in retrospect, they should have released at once. When firms have done something wrong or have discovered a problem that would be embarrassing to them, their instinct is often to pretend that everything is fine, to ignore the problem, and to reject any outside interference. Sometimes a firm's problems are undeniable. Think of how Union Carbide was pole-axed in 1984 by the Bhopal chemical disaster, which killed and maimed thousands of innocent citizens in India. In many other cases, however, firms go to great lengths to deny that anything is wrong, even though they know that they have acted illegally or immorally. Think of all the firms that have knowingly dumped toxic wastes and have saved millions of dollars in clean-up costs for the firm's owners by transferring those costs to the environment. These were cases where $U > R$ because the firms confidently expected not to be caught — or to suffer only minimal sanctions if they were.

Firms misbehave like this because top managers quickly calculate that their Upside is significant if they can only get away with fixing the problem before anyone outside the firm notices that something is wrong. For one thing, they are unlikely to face pressure to resign; for another, they might save large sums if they do not have to take responsibility for their misdeeds. During this phase of behavior, firms are assigning a low value to lambda. They are risk takers either because they are gambling on a positive outcome or because they are not considering scenarios under which things could get really bad. Hence, they underestimate their Regret. For the same reason, firms will often try to cover up bad things — always a risky course. (Think of the high proportion of whistle-blowers who are relatively junior in their organizations. Perhaps they will have less Regret than their bosses if their revelations cause damage to the reputation and value of the firm.) If bad things eventually become public, the firm and its senior managers are exposed to serious Regret, at which point the managers stand to lose their jobs anyway. At this stage, firms tend to become highly risk averse. Their value for lambda climbs sharply because they are now concerned about managing the downside. They can also see, close up, the danger of not considering scenarios under which they might suffer worse than they are already suffering.

Lambda is by no means the end of our risk management story. Recall that we set out the equation $U - R$ to represent how we can view risk in a way that takes into account the Upside as well as Regret? That calculation gives us, in effect, a picture of the net performance of a portfolio or investment. It is "net" because we have adjusted our Upside to take into account the risks that might lead to Regret. In Chapter 7, we will explain how we can measure risk-adjusted performance and why this has often proved to be an elusive notion in the real world.

First, however, let's look at a couple of other examples in which U – R might have played a useful role at the time, but can also offer a convincing explanation after the event. As we write this book, Swiss banks are struggling to recover from a disastrous period during which their role as conduits for Nazi gold during World War II has been exposed. In fact, there were two strands to their problem. The first stemmed from the fact that they shamelessly benefited from Swiss neutrality. Not only was German gold stored, but also much wealth was passed on to German allies by Swiss banks that were famous for their secrecy and discretion. In addition, a second damaging strand was often conflated with the first—it became apparent that Swiss banks were sitting on large amounts of money that belonged to victims of the Nazi Holocaust. Stirred by aggressive politicians in America, relatives of Holocaust victims became much more vocal than they had been in the past about claiming lost inheritances.

This was emotive stuff. If they had thought hard about their downside at the outset, the banks might quickly have come to a decision to do their best to research and pay up on any valid claims, and to open their books to independent outsiders' scrutiny. The prospect of aged Jewish claimants making headlines because they had been rebuffed yet again by a mighty and arrogant Swiss bank was not a pleasant one.

Instead, the banks embarked on a course of slow self-torture. As their defense against charges of aiding and abetting smugglers of Nazi gold, they bluntly and self-righteously pointed out that other commercial and central banks were scarcely blameless. This was true. It emerged, for instance, that even such an august institution as the Bank of England was sitting on a fortune in Nazi gold, taken in full knowledge of its allies as retribution at the end of the war. In addition, America's Federal Reserve Bank in New York had melted down Nazi gold bars so that their origins would be disguised. However, for the Swiss banks' critics, this was mere fog—a blatant attempt to divert attention from the real issue.

As for the claims of Holocaust victims, the banks had always said that most claimants could not offer sufficient proof that their dead relatives had indeed had Swiss bank accounts. Besides, no documents existed that would throw light on the matter. This was exposed as hogwash. Many claimants were able to show how they had systematically been ignored or mistreated since the end of the war. Over a period of months in 1996, the Swiss banks were embarrassed by a series of revelations. The biggest own-goal was scored by Union Bank of Switzerland, which sacked a security guard who had bravely rescued a bundle of old documents from destruction and handed them over to an outside body. The very bank that had denied the existence of such documents was furtively and perhaps dishonestly shredding papers that might have validated survivors' claims.

This and other horrors had to come to light before the banks began to change their tune. Lasting damage had been done to their collective reputations. Swiss banking had been synonymous with respect and integrity. Not any longer. How could the banks have been so stupid? Arrogance provides a partial answer. But a more satisfactory response is to challenge their risk management skills. Had they performed an honest $U - R$ analysis, they would have seen that they stood to lose a great deal but had very little to gain. In fact, the amounts of money at stake in the form of unclaimed deposits appear to have been relatively small—perhaps a few tens of millions of dollars, depending on how interest for the intervening years is charged. The amount lost by the Swiss banks because of their damaged image will probably turn out to very large indeed. Swiss banks have already been excluded from the banking syndicates that raise money for American cities and states—a move that, if it becomes widespread, could end up costing the banks hundreds of millions of dollars. Interestingly, the banks have gradually changed their position over time, in an effort to become more open and responsive to pressures from outside. But they did so too late. By the time their lambda altered so that they were genuinely risk averse, their names were already mud. Only when the extent of the damage was becoming clear did the banks consider that extremely nasty scenarios might occur. If they had done so sooner, they might have averted much of the damage that they are experiencing. Theirs is a classic case of extrapolating past indifference into the future, and failing to see tomorrow.

Earlier, we mentioned that someone offered a partnership must consider both the rewards and the costs because with a share of a partnership's equity comes an equal share of the liabilities. If you thought that one of your potential partners was a profligate spendthrift, you might think twice about assuming his or her liabilities, even if the rewards were tempting.

But what if you were a partner at an established firm and some of your colleagues proposed changing the firm's ownership structure so that it became a public company? How might you make this calculation? That is exactly what happened in 1996 at Goldman, Sachs, one of the world's top investment banks and one of the last remaining partnerships on Wall Street. (The only other one of note is Brown Brothers Harriman, a tiny firm compared to Goldman.) The decision to float the firm as a public company was put to a vote of partners. The idea had the support of some of the firm's senior figures, including its managing partner. Why did these partners want to float Goldman? They thought that the interests of the firm would be best served if it could freely raise money in the public equity market. Investment banking had changed from a parochial business that required very little capital to a global enterprise with a voracious appetite for money that was used as a cushion for the in-house risk taking that had become routine. Goldman had periodically raised capital privately by selling small bits of its equity to one–off investors. But the senior partners thought they needed the greater speed and flexibility offered by going public. Moreover, because they were regularly reporting record earnings, it seemed a fine time to sell the firm for a fat price. They could see plenty of Upside and very little Regret! Small wonder they embarked on a powerful campaign within Goldman to lobby voting partners.

To their amazement and frustration, they lost the vote. They had failed to see that their junior colleagues, each of whom had a vote, would make quite different $U - R$ calculations. The key to understanding the voting is to know that it takes time for a Goldman partner to accumulate wealth. Each year, provided the firm makes a net profit, a share of the rewards is attributed to each partner. Much of this wealth is not taken as salary but must be retained within the firm as equity. Even after partners retire, they often must wait for years before they can get their hands on their equity in the form of cash. And even though junior partners earn fabulous salaries by most people's standards, they know that even bigger rewards are slowly building up over the years. If Goldman were to go public, the senior partners stood to turn their illiquid equity into a liquid investment that they could then turn into cash by selling. They would be seriously rich, but in a more attractive vehicle than at present. But the junior partners would receive far smaller amounts of shares because they have not yet built up much equity. Their big years are still ahead of them. And they foresaw a further problem. In a public market, the value of the firm could be adversely affected by the cashing out of senior partners, something that would then directly affect their wealth. If Goldman remained a partnership, they would be protected by the rules governing how and when retiring partners can convert their shares into cash. Many of the junior partners were all too conscious that the firm had been enjoying some remarkably fat years, producing profits that were probably not repeatable forever. By the time they were senior partners themselves, they might welcome the cushion that would be there because earnings in prior good years had been retained in the business. Thus, although there was undoubtedly some Upside for them in the event of a flotation, the junior partners could see plenty of Regret, to the point that most of them voted against the proposal.

This episode exposed a risk that had been overlooked by Goldman's senior partners: a difference in timing of partners' rewards could make it structurally impossible to realize a consensus on going public. The firm was in a curious position. Its oldest and wisest heads thought one course of action was in the firm's best interests, and could also see plenty of personal Upside. In their case, any Regret lay in their perception of the firm's diminishing ability to compete while it remained a partnership. But the younger and more headstrong group saw only diminished personal Upside. They could not look beyond their narrow personal interests to the broader interests of the firm because they felt too much Regret in the event that the firm's structure altered.

The Goldman case had even more complications. For instance, the option of floating as a public company carried big implications for the firm's culture of risk and reward. As a partnership, outrageous rewards accompanied success. Becoming a partner traditionally meant guaranteed financial wealth beyond most people's dreams. No wonder Goldman had fostered a culture of intense competition. For every new partner, there would be several talented and motivated employees who failed to make the grade, many of whom would subsequently leave to take senior jobs elsewhere. The Upside was so tempting that plenty of people were willing to live with the Regret of failure; after all, they were being well compensated while trying. Thus, below the junior, most recently elected, partners was a secondary level of employees who also felt greatly threatened by the proposed flotation. What would happen to their goal of becoming a partner if Goldman no longer had such a rank because it was now public? More importantly, wouldn't the huge financial rewards of partnership be watered down, under pressure from external shareholders? This cadre—those who aspired to partnership in a few years' time—felt surprisingly negative about a flotation. And, in a fascinating way, their attitude strengthened the resolve of the junior partners, who would do best if Goldman continued to attract the brightest and most talented people—presuming they could turn their skills into profits. If the lack of the partnership incentive encouraged many of the brightest to take their skills elsewhere, then the junior partners' own prospects would be hurt. Suddenly, it no longer seems so strange that Goldman is still a partnership! Indeed, one wonders: How might Goldman ever change? Perhaps the partners' voting structure gave more weight to seniority; for example, a 20-year partner might have, say, five votes versus a three-year partner's single vote. Then the interests of the senior partners might hold sway. However, it is difficult to see why the junior partners would ever approve such a change. It would be tantamount to signing away a big chunk of their future Upside!

Another example of how a risk-adjusted framework explains people's behavior can be drawn from the world of publishing. Think how a publisher goes about rewarding its authors. Should it offer a $1 million advance (we wish!)? If it does, it had better realize significant Upside. Otherwise, it is likely to suffer large Regret. Publishers gauge how much they can pay as an advance by making what amounts to a risk-adjusted calculation. They need to attract and retain authors, so they must be prepared to pay some money up front—a premium, if you will. They know that if they pay a specific advance, incur normal production costs, and sell a certain number of copies, they will break even. If they have multiple printings and sell many more additional copies, they stand to reap considerable returns.

But the potential downside is large. Pay too big an advance and the publisher is almost guaranteed to suffer a loss. Small publishers experience this problem acutely. They have a higher value for lambda because a single costly mistake could wipe them out. Large houses try to create a portfolio of books and authors, diversifying their risk on any one project. When they think a book could become a best-seller, they can become surprisingly risk seeking, often spending large sums on marketing and promotion in order to enhance a book's prospects. They also make decisions that are difficult to defend using a risk-adjusted analysis. Some first-time pulp novelists—and occasionally, overhyped business writers—win huge advances. A publisher, envisioning sufficient Upside, may be willing to pay a crazy amount for the rights to, say, a book on a hot topic—the Internet, or Silicon Valley. A hot manuscript is the equivalent of a lottery ticket. There is no guarantee of a payoff for the publisher. But because the publisher thinks its skills will increase the chances of the book's success, it assigns the project a high market value. Because readers' tastes can be unpredictable, many of the costliest books fail to return publishers' investments. The game goes on because occasional payoffs are spectacular. Think of low-key books such as *Longitude* or *Boom, Bust and Echo*, which have become unexpected hits and have made fortunes for their publishers as well as their authors.

We hope it is becoming clear that the combination of Upside, Regret, and lambda is a powerful arsenal for thinking about decisions and analyzing problems. The methodology is interesting because it offers guidance on very specific and somewhat narrow problems (Which fund should I buy?) as well as on broad matters of strategy and investing (Should we float the firm or settle that lawsuit?). The range of examples we have found suggests that our risk management framework is as flexible as it is helpful.

Chapter 7

THE RAP TRAP
AND EVALUATIONS

In Chapter 4, we introduced lambda (λ) as a measure that helps to capture our changing appetites for risk. To illustrate the idea, we showed how we might view three different mutual funds, depending on our tolerance for risk. At present, it seems a distant dream to imagine that we could select real mutual funds in this way. The mutual fund revolution that has swept America and Canada, and is expected to change the structure of savings and investment in Europe and Japan in the future, has been profound, but it has its limits. And one of those limits forms the basis of this chapter. Remarkably, it is nearly impossible to make rational choices among funds, based on the information that is publicly available today.

We think that we can begin to meet this need, while using the idea of choosing between funds as the primary example of the next step in our risk management framework. If we are to assess risks meaningfully, then we need a way of adjusting what actually happens for the risk we have taken in order to expose ourselves to that outcome. The goal is risk-adjusted performance (RAP) measurement on the one hand; we need a technique that properly accounts for the risks that we have taken. On the other hand, to be consistent with our forward-looking view of risk, we also need a way of assessing our likely future risk-adjusted performance. How something performed on a risk-adjusted basis in the past does not tell us all we need to know if we are to make smart choices for tomorrow.

Mutual funds represent an ideal way of exploring these issues. It has become common wisdom these days that mutual funds represent a sensible way to save. Over time, they should yield higher returns than the old-style bank accounts into which people used to deposit their money unthinkingly. Moreover, because they pool the money of many investors, mutual funds can efficiently achieve diversification with lower transaction costs. For most people, they are a way of achieving higher returns while assuming less risk than if they were to hold stocks and bonds directly. This has proved particularly compelling for the cohort of baby boomers, who are concerned with providing adequately for their retirement. In their need for high returns, they have adopted risk profiles that suggest that they attach a relatively low value to lambda.

The growth of mutual funds has not all been smooth sailing. In the mid-1990s, American banks were rapped on the knuckles by regulators when it became apparent that many of the customers to whom they were trying to sell mutual funds believed that their investments would be covered by bank deposit insurance. Even today, in many American bank branches, the separation of insured and uninsured areas is less than explicit, and many consumers still mistakenly think that investment products they purchase at a bank will be insured. More generally, amid rising stock markets and a widespread sense that economic good times can roll on for many years, people don't seem to want to see banner headlines reminding them that mutual funds can actually go down in value. (We will show why that thought should be at the front of people's minds.)

Similarly, several big American money market funds that competed heavily for people's short-term assets were embarrassed in 1994 when it emerged that they had been taking inappropriate risks in order to boost their returns. These "funds on steroids" were technically under water—the value of their assets was less than the notional $1 per share principal amount. Afraid of a mass revolt by consumers, fund management firms chose to bail out funds that had broken the buck.

Financial risk taking through mutual funds has become a common pursuit. This has brought great benefits—a generation of investors has found an efficient vehicle in which to ride a great bull market in financial assets. Returns have been far more broadly spread than in the past. At the same time, changes in welfare and retirement benefit systems are putting greater pressure on individuals to fend for themselves. Many workers can no longer rely on a definite amount when they retire, but must take their chances in "defined contribution" plans, which invest in the markets (often via mutual funds) and deliver an uncertain payoff at the moment of retirement. How our mutual funds perform is therefore not an academic issue, but one that could define how well or how modestly we will live in retirement. The latter point is often missed. If our funds perform below our expectations, we might be unable to take that cruise to the Caribbean or buy those new titanium golf clubs. When we embrace risk in search of returns, we also expose ourselves to Regret if things don't work out.

In the days before the mutual fund boom, few investors bothered to ask too many questions about funds' performance. The funds generally reported their historical total returns and left it to investors to figure out whether they were a good bet. Unfortunately, most investors simply did not have sufficient information to make a rational decision. Not only are historical total returns inadequate as a guide to the future, but also they tell us nothing about the riskiness of individual funds.

Moreover, there can be significant hidden risks in mutual fund investing. Choosing a fund used to be simple enough, but there is now a bewildering array of funds from which to choose, and reams of information about each of those funds. Fund managers know a good trend when they see one, and the past few years have brought a plethora of new funds. Many attempt a degree of specialization that would have been unthinkable a few years ago. For instance, American investors can put money into the Pauve Tombstone Fund—an index fund that tracks the nine public firms that are engaged in the business of death, whether through funeral homes and cemetery management, casket and headstone manufacture, or burial insurance. The fund, launched in mid-1997, claims that its investment style has handily outperformed the Dow Jones Industrial Average and the S&P 500—among other leading indexes. The performance numbers used for its promotion were based on a notional index that had been tracked back to 1986 and relied on a sixfold increase in a single stock for much of its impressive record!

Another hidden risk is that funds and their managers are not always what they seem. On the face of it, mutual fund managers should have exactly the same interests as the customers who pay them to manage their money. After all, the better they perform, the more profit they stand to make and the happier their investors will be. Reality is not so simple. One academic study has neatly demonstrated that mutual funds suffer from their own version of "moral hazard"—that is, they can be tempted by perverse incentives to act in their own interests at the expense of existing customers' interests.

The key to the moral hazard, as well as to the idea of risk-adjusted performance, is to understand one of the basic tenets of modern portfolio theory—the level of absolute return achieved by a fund depends on how much risk it takes. Successful funds grow by performing well, which swells existing assets under management but also helps to attract new investors. The "hottest" funds attract the most new cash. Plenty of academic studies have shown that investors do indeed tend to "chase" performance in this way, even though there is no rational long-term justification for such behavior.

Because fund companies' rewards are based on how much money they manage, they clearly have a strong incentive to bring in new customers. But what if funds adjust how much risk they take in order to maximize their chances of attracting that new cash? This would involve taking more risk if the fund has been underperforming, or less risk if a period of overperformance might be jeopardized by a subsequent change of fortune.

The logical point to alter a fund's risk profile in either direction would be in the run up to a deadline for performance measurement—a moment that defines the fund's position relative to other funds and sets its ability to market itself to new customers. September marks the beginning of the final quarter of funds' annual performance marathon.

How might this practice harm existing investors? Their interests are served when the fund maximizes its risk-adjusted returns at all times. A fund that has more than half an eye on attracting new money might make decisions that undermine this approach. Thus, investors might miss out on performance that the fund had chosen to forgo because it had previously done well. Alternatively, a fund might assume more risk than its investors are comfortable with—a phenomenon that upset the money market fund industry during 1994, when it became known that many funds were using risky derivatives to try to boost returns.

Judith Chevalier and Glenn Ellison, economists at the University of Chicago and MIT respectively, looked at a sample of American growth and income equity funds over the period from 1982 to 1992, and found that there were indeed such changes in funds' risk taking. In particular, the period from September to the funds' year-end in December was characterized by risk taking that confirms the perverse effects of the incentives described above.

For now, there is not much that mutual fund investors can do to avoid or lessen this moral hazard, apart perhaps from sticking to so-called closed-end funds, which seek simply to grow existing assets. But the Chevalier–Ellison study is a reminder that funds are not always the straightforward investment option they might appear to be. A powerful conflict can occur if the two parties to a contract have different Upside and Regret. For the fund manager, the Upside from bringing in new money is bigger than the Upside from chasing more performance. In this case, the existing returns are seen as sufficient to pull in new investors, so why take more risk? After all, that would only increase the fund manager's Regret.

For existing investors, however, Upside is a simpler notion. They want the best possible performance as defined by their funds' investment goals. They will suffer from Regret if their fund manager becomes risk averse for his or her own reasons. And this is not just because they might lose some Upside returns. A change of behavior by one fund can have powerful (and largely unseen) effects on the risk profile of their overall portfolio.

Perhaps unsurprisingly, there is growing demand for better ways of measuring how much risk funds are assuming. Early in 1995, the Securities and Exchange Commission called for industry comments on how to improve risk disclosure for mutual funds. After much feedback—some 3,600 individual investors responded, and an additional 600 investors were professionally surveyed—SEC chairman Arthur Levitt made the following feeble announcement: ". . . we do not need to mandate a specific risk measure." But he also said that funds should try to clarify their investment style in their marketing literature, and should show their recent historical performance via a simple bar chart.

The special survey that accompanied the SEC's research was organized by the Investment Company Institute (ICI), the American mutual fund industry's trade body. Like the SEC, the ICI was in the end unconvinced regarding the need for a risk measure. But in interviews with around 650 investors, the ICI made some interesting findings. In particular, it showed that when investors are allowed to talk about risk in their own words, they use language that is eerily reminiscent of our risk framework. For instance, the two most common risk characteristics that mutual fund investors mentioned were "loss of money" and "gain relative to chance of loss." Each of these terms sounds like Regret or risk-adjusted return by another name (see Table 7.1).

When the interviewees were prompted with a list of risk concepts, nearly one-third of them picked four or more different factors—demonstrating, concluded the ICI, that "risk is a multifaceted concept." An impressive 57 percent of the sample defined risk to include the chance of losing some of their original investment (Regret); nearly half were concerned about at least keeping pace with inflation (see Table 7.2).

TABLE 7.1
*Recent Buyers' Characterization of Mutual Fund
Risk, in Their Own Words**

	Percent of Respondents
Chance or risk of losing money (net)	51
Loss of original investment	30
Chance of losing money, size of potential loss	20
Losing money in the short term, immediate loss of money	2
Chance of an investment not keeping pace with inflation	1
The chance of making money and the chance of losing money (net)	26
Taking risk for a possible gain, potential for higher gains	14
Chance for a gain or a loss	13
Volatility, effects of the market (net)	7
Swings in the value of an investment	6
Market fluctuations, volatility of the stock market	2
Not realizing a return on my investment	6
Stability of the investment or the investment company (net)	3
Financial stability of the sponsoring company	1
Mutual funds safer than other types of investment	1
Mutual funds not insured investment	1
Not having enough money at the end of the investment horizon to achieve financial goals	2
All investments have risks	6
Other	8

Number of respondents = 637.

*All open-ended responses with similar meanings were grouped together. Some respondents indicated more than one characteristic; multiple responses are included. A "net" is an aggregation of subcategories where responders are only counted once, regardless of multiple responses across subcategories.

Source: ICI.

TABLE 7.2
*Concepts Included in Recent Buyers' Definition of
Mutual Fund Risk*

	Percent of Respondents
*The chance of . . .**	
Losing some of the original investment	57
Mutual fund investments' not keeping pace with inflation	47
The value of mutual fund investments fluctuating up and down	46
Not having enough money at the end of the investment horizon to achieve goals	40
The income distributed by the fund declining	38
Mutual fund investments not performing as a bank CD	30
Mutual fund investments not performing as well as an index	27
Losing money within the first year	23
Respondents indicating . . .	
One concept	16
Two concepts	29
Three concepts	25
Four or more concepts	30

Number of respondents = 648.
*Multiple responses included.
Source: ICI.

From these findings, one might have concluded that investors' awareness of risk is hopelessly at odds with the marketing strategies of the entire mutual fund industry. In other words, while investors talk about risk and the danger of losses, they are constantly bombarded with the impression that their funds can only increase in value. Unfortunately, however, the ICI had a different understanding of its research. It took the fact that investors seemed to be well aware of risk to mean that there was no need for a big shakeup of risk disclosure. In particular, it found that because a relatively small number of investors was making use of numerical and technical descriptions of risk, it would be better to stick with simple bar charts showing annual returns.

This reporting method, and especially the SEC's unwillingness to adopt an aggressive stance, rightly did not satisfy everybody. In July 1996, when a group of leading financial economists met to discuss the issue of risk disclosure by mutual funds, they made several important points. First, because it is complicated to calculate the effect of one mutual fund on an investor's overall portfolio, it is indeed unlikely that a single measure of risk will be adequate. For that reason, it is not good enough to review how a fund has performed in the past, even if that review includes how much the fund's returns have varied around its benchmark. "Investors and their advisors need information that can enable them to assess sources of future risk: in many cases, history may not be the best guide to the future." (Remember, too, the risk elements that make up our paradigm. Risk lies ahead of us, not behind us.)

The economists went on to make some familiar but important observations about risk. Investors' primary need is "to predict the likely range of a fund's return in the future. The greater is this range, the more risky are a fund's prospects."

Further:

Investments in funds are risky because they are exposed to economic forces or factors for which the future is uncertain. Some of these are unique to individual funds, but many are common to many funds. Thus, a U.S. stock fund will typically move to a greater or lesser extent with the overall U.S. stock market. A fund's risk depends on how closely its return is coupled with given indexes, the riskiness of each index, and how closely the indexes tend to move together.

In other words, we need to peer at the risk-adjusted details beyond a fund's headline returns. We also need to view funds in their proper context. As we shall see, there is little point in measuring funds' risk-adjusted performance if we do not also view the wider picture of risk and re-ward. Observing what we need to do is simple enough; doing it is more complicated.

Squaring the Risk Circle

Complicated, but not impossible. One of the thinkers leading the way in RAP measures is Franco Modigliani, the Nobel prize winner we mentioned in Chapter 2, and presently a professor emeritus at MIT. Even more curiously, he is exploiting a unique family connection. His granddaughter Leah is a researcher in the equity division at Morgan Stanley Dean Witter, an investment bank. Spurred by her bosses' interest in accounting for risks as well as returns, she has worked with her grandfather on a risk-adjusted measure (informally known as M^2) that allows investors to compare individual funds as well as broader sectors and indexes.

Is this obviously a good thing? We think so (even though we have a slightly different approach ourselves). Existing performance numbers and rankings give investors either a partial or a misleading picture.

It is crazy that this should be the case, but it is simple enough to prove. Earlier, we mentioned the ICI study, in which three-quarters of those sampled mentioned past performance as a reason for buying a fund. In 1995 and 1996, three professors at Columbia University inter-viewed more than 3,000 investors and asked them what factors influ-enced their choices. The results showed overwhelmingly that past performance was relied on above all other indicators. On a scale of 1 (lowest) to 5 (highest), for instance, past performance scored 4.62. Fees scored a wimpish 2.28; investment style, 1.68; checking and brokerage services, 1.38. Confidentiality brought up the rear, at 1.35.

As noted in a more recent study by a consulting group at Smith Bar-ney, a brokerage firm, investors are presented with a strong message by the fund management industry and the media: "Choose the best performers." Morningstar, the Chicago-based firm that monitors mutual funds, rates funds by awarding them one to five stars. The better a fund has performed, the more stars it is likely to accumulate. And a quick glance at any newspaper's financial pages will show how firms seize on these stars as marketing manna. One research firm calculated that three-quarters of the new money that went into equity mutual funds in early 1996 was invested in funds that had either four or five stars from Morningstar.

The Smith Barney study examined whether fund managers are capable of consistently high performance. It looked at a sample of seventy-two fund managers who had ten-year records, tracked their returns over various time horizons, and then ranked them into groups. No matter which time horizon the study used, it found that the top performers in one period were, in the next period, more likely to become duffers than to repeat their good performance. As Table 7.3 shows, there was a strong correlation between underperformers in

TABLE 7.3
*Two-Year Performance Periods of Seventy-Two Stock Investment Managers**

| Manager's Rank | Average Two-Year Annualized Return | | Improvement or Deterioration in Performance |
	Initial Two Years	Subsequent Two Years	
Top	23.63%	13.89%	−9.73%
Second	18.01	15.18	−2.83
Third	14.81	15.35	+0.54
Fourth	12.47	15.72	+3.25
Bottom	6.95	17.71	+10.76

*Average of returns for managers in each quintile over all two-year periods from 1/1/87 through 12/31/96.
Source: Smith Barney.

one period and better performance in the next. Some of these findings are the result of the fund managers' investment styles; as they go in and out of favor with investors, their performance is affected. However, the overwhelming conclusion is that investors who rely on past performance (the majority) are doing so at their peril.

Fund companies give themselves wide latitude when it comes to publishing performance figures. Let's look at a real example of the problem faced by investors. Our unfortunate subject is the Babson Value Fund, chosen at random from a selection of mutual fund prospectuses. This fund's prospectus for March 31, 1997, contains a section, under the heading "Performance Comparisons," that speaks volumes about the problems of total return measurements and the deficiencies of existing rankings. By the way, the fund specializes in "common stocks considered undervalued." Here is how the section reads:

> In advertisements or in reports to shareholders, the Fund may compare its performance to that of other mutual funds with similar investment objectives and to stock or other relevant indices. For example, it may compare its performance to rankings prepared by Lipper Analytical Services Inc. (Lipper), a widely recognized independent service, which monitors the performance of mutual funds. The Fund may compare its performance to the Standard & Poor's 500 Stock Index (S&P 500), an index of unmanaged groups of common stocks, the Dow Jones Industrial Average, a recognized unmanaged index of common stocks of industrial companies listed on the NYSE, or the Consumer Price Index. Performance information, rankings, ratings, published editorial comments and listings as reported in national financial publications such as *Kiplinger's Personal Finance Magazine, Business Week, Morningstar Mutual Funds, Investor's Business Daily, Institutional Investor, The Wall Street Journal, Mutual Fund Forecaster, No-Load Investor, Money, Forbes, Fortune* and *Barron's* may also be used in comparing performance of the Fund. . . .

The section goes on to name fourteen additional magazines and newsletters that can be cited or used for comparison. When multiplied across the mutual fund industry, this amounts to a performance measurement farce. Any fund that generates reasonable total returns can expect some publication somewhere to comment on it or to rank it so that it appears to be a leader in what has become a crowded field. In the Babson example, the fund management is also giving itself wide discretion in picking the benchmark against which it might choose to compare performance—the S&P 500, the Dow, and the CPI. Presumably, it will pick whichever benchmark makes its performance look best and will advertise accordingly.

Our intention here is not to pick on Babson. It is merely an example—and far from the worst we could find—of the way the mutual fund business presently works against the interests of the very investors it relies on for its profits. It should be obvious from the lengthy list of newsletters and publications that there is no agreed-on method of ranking funds, whether for risk or anything else. Hence, perhaps, the stubborn persistence of the simplest total return measure as the basis of most performance measurement. The upshot is that funds can make claims that are extremely difficult for investors to unpack.

To confuse the picture, some rankings do attempt to adjust for risk. However, they all offer subjective or unhelpful approaches to risk and prove a poor basis for comparison. Morningstar, for instance, claims that it takes risk into account when it awards its stars. But let's say you are trying to compare two double-star funds. How can you know which one is the better risk-adjusted bet?

The M^2 measure draws on a simple idea that was inspired by the original Miller–Modigliani theorem: just as firms can alter their debt–equity ratio to adopt a risk profile, so any fund can be levered up or down so that it is equally risky in relation to a chosen benchmark (using volatility as a simple measure of risk, although any risk measure favored by an investor could be substituted). In other words, risk is not a fixed characteristic of a fund or portfolio; it can be changed, using leverage.

This is another simple but profound insight. It rests on the notion of *fungibility*. This strange financial word has nothing to do with mushrooms; it simply means "exchangeable" or "interchangeable." If something is fungible, it is, in effect, equivalent to something else. Equivalence and our ability to replicate something form the essence of how we reach a price for things. But this concept also works in another interesting way. For any portfolio, there is an equivalent simpler portfolio that has the same risk–reward characteristics but might contain a fraction of the assets—or different assets. By exploiting fungibility and equivalence, we can understand and manage our portfolios and assets with far greater precision.

For example, a risky technology mutual fund could be partially sold off in favor of Treasury bills until its volatility matches that of a benchmark such as the S&P 500. A low-risk bond fund would use a margin account (that is, borrowing) to create overinvestment until it too reached the same level of volatility as the benchmark. Bingo! Then the funds' performance can be measured on a risk-adjusted basis. If the risk-equivalent fund outperforms the benchmark, for instance, then it is an attractive option—it has returned more performance for the same level of risk. And its risk-adjusted performance can be directly compared to that of other funds. One must simply repeat the leverage calculation for each fund and compare it against the benchmark. A simple way to think of the measure is that it captures how efficiently a fund produces its returns. The more "efficient" a fund is, the less risk it needs to take in order to deliver a given level of return. For comparative purposes, a better way to think of the measure is that it ranks funds' returns as if they had all taken the same amount of risk.

The M^2 measure produces startling results. As Table 7.4 shows, some funds clearly take more risk in order to produce their returns. Fidelity's famous Magellan Fund (now closed to new money) has higher headline return numbers, but risk-sensitive investors would have had a better time buying the less-hyped Puritan Fund.

TABLE 7.4
M² Analysis of Selected Mutual Funds

Mutual Funds (in order of total return)	Ten-Year Average Annual Total Return	Risk-Adjusted Return (M²)	Risk-Adjusted Rank
Benchmark: S&P 500	15.2		
AIM Constellation	19.2	14.5	4
T. Rowe Price New Horizons	16.3	13.4	6
Fidelity Magellan	16.2	14.9	3
20th Century Vista Investors	15.2	11.9	7
Vanguard Windsor	14.0	13.8	5
Fidelity Puritan	12.5	15.7	2
Income Fund of America	12.2	16.9	1
T-Bill	5.6		

Based on quarterly returns, 10 years ending 96Q4.
Source for quarterly returns: Morningstar Inc.
Source: Morgan Stanley.

Moreover, the M² measure throws interesting light on existing industry rankings that purport to adjust for risk, such as *Business Week's* annual survey (Table 7.5). From a sample of small cap funds, FPA Capital achieved the best risk-adjusted returns and earned more than Heartland's fund in 1996. But its *Business Week* ranking for that year puts it well below its less efficient rival, suggesting that the risk measure being used is not capturing satisfactorily the funds' risk taking.

If they apply it broadly, investors can use the M² technique to select funds that are efficient risk takers. They can compare benchmarks. In Table 7.5, for instance, the S&P 500 offered better risk-adjusted returns than the Russell 2000 index of small company shares. That may not surprise many professional investors. But unsophisticated investors might think mistakenly that small companies always give higher returns because they carry higher risks. There can be periods when that is not true, and we happen to be coming out of one such period. Using a measure

TABLE 7.5
Small Cap Funds versus S&P 500

	Total Returns*	M²	BW Overall		BW Category
FPA Capital	24.5	14.2	↑	Avg	Sm Cap Value
Heartland	22.0	13.6	↑↑↑	↑↑	Sm Cap Value
AIM Aggressive Growth	24.9	13.0	↓	↑↑	Sm Cap Growth
PIMCO Adv Opportunity C	21.3	11.5	↓↓	Avg	Sm Cap Growth
American Cent—20thC Giftrust	20.8	10.0	↓↓↓	↓	Sm Cap Growth
Russell 2000 Index	15.0	12.4	—		
S&P 500 Index	15.2	15.2	—		

*Over 5 years.
Sources: Morgan Stanley, *Business Week.*

such as M^2 might help investors to feel more comfortable: they can deliberately select a relatively risky fund, as opposed to merely guessing, as they must today. In other words, even after making an M^2 calculation, an investor might choose the risky technology fund, but will do so with a clear sense of its relative riskiness to other technology funds as well as to a benchmark.

Unfortunately, however, even M^2 suffers from the significant drawback that it relies on past performance figures. Investors are better off with the measure than without it, but they must hope that funds stick to their established risk-taking habits. If a manager leaves for another fund, or if markets change, then their investments might turn out quite differently. As one leading mutual fund analyst puts it, there is a huge gap between nice theories about performance measurement and the complex realities of the marketplace. Indeed, the one common and honest piece of disclosure in mutual fund marketing literature is that past performance (including risk-adjusted performance) is not a guide to the future!

In most situations in which financial decisions have to be made, the outcomes are typically more complicated than simply an Upside or a downside. There are many possible scenarios involving future events, and often it is not clear ahead of time which of these will result in gains or losses. Still, as we will show, these more complex decisions can be collapsed into a decision involving Upside and downside only, and can be valued, as we did previously, by comparing the Upside to the value of a bet and the downside to the cost of insurance.

Assume we wish to compute a forward-looking measure of risk for a mutual fund. One possible way (but by no means the only one) to do this is described as follows.

Today, we know a couple of things about the typical mutual fund. We know its absolute returns. And we can calculate easily enough how volatile it has been against a chosen benchmark such as the S&P 500 index. This measure, known as Beta (ß), has been explained in Chapter 3. As this entire book argues, however, we need risk management rules that respond to some basic observations. Risk is a forward-looking concept, and it can change in the future. Similarly, a fund's Beta can have one value today and a quite different one in the future. To see this, we only need to understand that, measured against the same benchmark, a mutual fund is capable of performing very differently in the coming six months than in the past six months.

Using the rules of modern finance theory—specifically, an approach known as the Capital-Asset Pricing Model (CAPM)—we would compute the change in value of the fund as Beta times the change in index value. For example, say we were looking at an American mutual fund that invests in domestic equities. We might then say that the fund's risk is measured by its Beta to the S&P index. High Betas imply high risk, and low Betas indicate low risk.

However, in a forward-looking world, Betas will not stay the same. We have seen from past experience that Betas can change over time, just as the degree to which the fund outperforms or underperforms the index changes with time. Backward-looking measures would take Beta to be constant. Forward-looking measures would assume that there are some scenarios in which Beta could increase in value, and other scenarios in which Beta would decrease in value. In a forward-looking measure, Beta is not constant but varies from scenario to scenario.

We do not expect the index to stay constant. It will vary too. In some cases, there is the possibility that it will decline in value; in others, it will increase in value.

The key to our choice of scenarios is that we take into account all the possible values (even extreme moves) of both Beta and the index. To keep our calculations simple, we will assume that the only things that affect our fund and the index are the possible ways in which Beta could vary and the possible ways in which the index could gain or lose value.

For example, let's assume that our fund has a mark-to-market value of 100 today, and that its Beta with respect to the S&P has been calculated to be 2. In the past, we have seen this fund's Beta move between 1.5 and 4. The index, on the other hand, has been as low as 80 and as high as 130 over the past year. A set of scenarios follows.

TABLE 7.6
Outcomes of Various Scenarios

Beta	Index Value	Index Value	Change in Fund Value	Probability (%)	Change in Fund – Change in Index
1.5	80	−20	−30	3	−10
1.5	100	0	0	15	0
1.5	130	30	45	12	15
2.0	80	−20	−40	6	−20
2.0	100	0	0	30	0
2.0	130	30	60	24	30
4.0	80	−20	−80	1	−60
4.0	100	0	0	5	0
4.0	130	30	120	4	90

Using the equation, change in fund value = Beta × Change in the index value, we get the scenario outcomes shown in Table 7.6. It helps to rank the outcomes from best to worst, so that we can see how much returns might vary under different scenarios.

Table 7.7 interprets these numbers. The worst possible performance of this fund relative to the benchmark is a loss of 60 (i.e., a 60 percent loss in value relative to the starting value of 100) with a probability of 1 percent. This is the maximum Regret. The best possible performance relative to the benchmark is a gain of 90 (a 90 percent increase) with a probability of 4 percent. This is the maximum Upside.

How might an investor decide on the basis of these numbers? Remember that we have chosen very simple scenarios; in a real test we could choose very complex ones that are related to our primary concerns and expectations. Even in this simple case, however, we can notice that the fund is likely to perform well if its relationship to the market stays broadly the same and the market is steady. Under those conditions, it has a 30 percent chance of performing in line with the index. But if the market does well, the fund has nearly a one in four chance of outperforming the index significantly.

TABLE 7.7
Interpretation of Fund Performance

Beta	Index Value	Probability (%)	Change in Fund – Change in Index
4	130	4	90
2	130	24	30
1.5	130	12	15
4	100	5	0
2	100	30	0
1.5	100	15	0
1.5	80	3	−10
2	80	6	−20
4	80	1	−60

We expect the adoption of forward-looking measures to result in an increased interest by investors in the scenarios used to compute them. We expect to see measures published along with the scenario assumptions that were used to compute them.

We also expect that standard sets of scenarios for marking-to-future calculations will be made available commercially. And an interesting outgrowth of these measures will be the insurance that investors and fund managers will be able to offer together with the funds. The Regret measure is the cost of insuring the downside. We expect to see "insurance" contracts, in the form of customized put options, being offered to protect all or part of the downside of a fund. For example, an out-of-the-money contract could protect all downside beyond a 10 percent drop in value. We also expect to see call options on funds, for they are precisely the forward-looking Upside of a fund. A range forward contract (the kind we mentioned in Chapter 5) would give a fraction of the Upside of a fund at no premium and with no downside.

Scenarios will be easy to describe and will be more easily understood by all investors (see Figure 7.1). A forward-looking paradigm eliminates the need for arcane formulas and risk measurement methods that nobody without a PhD in nuclear physics can understand. There will be no need to fly blind anymore! Or, more precisely, there will be no need to ask investors to drive cars that have only rearview mirrors.

To Buy or Not to Buy

The absence of a Marking-to-Future approach is keenly felt elsewhere. To illustrate this, let's consider the decision we face when we are thinking about whether to buy a house and how we should finance the transaction.

Assume you have purchased a $100,000 house and have agreed to a closing date six months from now. Interest rates are currently

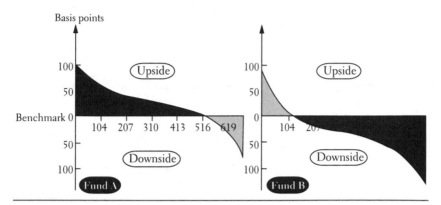

FIGURE 7.1   Mark-to-future: Best and worst mutual funds. These graphs show how two mutual funds perform in a variety of scenarios. The vertical axis shows the degree to which each fund either outperforms or underperforms the benchmark. The horizontal axis represents the scenarios ordered from most to least advantageous. Several hundred scenarios are taken into account. The shaded areas show the value of Upside and Downside. These figures reveal at a glance that Fund A is better than Fund B because its risk-adjusted return is greater.

10 percent, and your bank is prepared to guarantee you a mortgage at 12 percent per annum starting at the closing date, if you commit to the deal. The $12,000 per annum charge, if you accept the bank's offer, is just about what you can afford with your current salary. Interest rates have been dropping for the past few months, and there is a chance they could drop further—at least that's what many market analysts are predicting. If they drop further, your mortgage costs would be lower if you can delay the financing.

There is always a chance that the analysts are wrong and rates will rise, in which case you might pay a higher rate if you delay financing for six months. You believe there is a 60 percent chance that interest rates will fall to 5 percent in six months; a 20 percent chance they will remain the same; and a 20 percent chance they will rise to 20 percent (Figure 7.2).

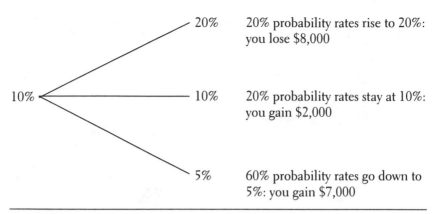

20%

20% probability rates rise to 20%: you lose $8,000

10%

10%

20% probability rates stay at 10%: you gain $2,000

5%

60% probability rates go down to 5%: you gain $7,000

FIGURE 7.2 **Scenario diagram for financing your house purchase over a six-month period.**

The way to evaluate this decision is to determine the consequences of the two alternatives. Under alternative one (commit to financing now), your cost in six months' time will be 12 percent of $100,000, or $12,000 per annum. This is your cost regardless of what happens to interest rates. There is no risk in this strategy. Alternative two (finance later) carries some risk, but could result in a much lower financing cost if the analysts are correct. If rates go up, your annual mortgage fee could be as high as $20,000. If rates stay the same, your costs would be $10,000 per annum. If rates go down, your annual cost could be as low as $5,000!

Relative to alternative one, you will suffer an $8,000 loss if rates go up ($12,000 vs. $20,000). If rates stay the same, you will gain $2,000 per annum; you will be able to finance at $10,000 whereas you would have paid $12,000 per annum if you had accepted the bank's offer today. If rates go down, you will gain $7,000 per annum by not taking the bank's offer.

Analysts are predicting that rates are likely to drop. Should you wait to finance the mortgage?

Two of the three possible scenarios offer a combined 80 percent chance that you will gain between $2,000 and $7,000. The third scenario offers a 20 percent chance that you will lose $8,000. (On average, the gain would be $5,750 with an 80 percent likelihood. To see this, notice that you gain either $7,000 with a 60 percent probability, or $2,000 with a 20 percent probability. This averages out to $5,750 because, when you gain, three-fourths of the time the gain will be $7,000, and one-fourth of the time it will be $2,000.)

Following the method we described in Chapter 6, if the risk-adjusted value of this deal is positive, you would prefer to wait and not take the bank's offer. (Remember that we are calculating all figures relative to the alternative of accepting the bank's offer to lock in a financing rate today.) The risk-adjusted value would be the difference between what you would pay for a bet to win $5,750 with 80 percent certainty and the amount you would pay to insure a loss of $8,000 that could occur with 20 percent certainty.

One person would pay more for the bet than the value they would associate with the insurance. This means that they would not accept the bank's offer and would take their chances. Another person might feel differently if faced with your decision, especially if a $20,000 per annum mortgage is far more than he or she can afford. The extra $8,000 per annum might force that person to sell the house. To insure against such a loss, he or she might be willing to accept a much higher premium than you would. That person's risk-adjusted value would then be negative, and he or she would prefer the bank's alternative of a sure rate today.

Even though this deal involved more than two scenarios, we were able to reduce the problem to a choice between an Upside and a downside. This same approach can be applied to many other scenarios. It is always possible to reduce an analysis to examination of an Upside and a downside. The only controversial part of this analysis is the way in which we averaged across the two scenarios in which there was an Upside. Some people might prefer to phrase the Upside as the chance of winning between $2,000 and $7,000 with 80 percent certainty; in this way, it would not be an approximation. But, either way, the analysis does not change.

In general, the uncertainty about the future period over which risk is to be measured can be expressed in terms of scenarios. Scenarios can become quite complex combinations of things. In the above case, at the end of six months, you should take into account the possible changes in the price of housing as well as in the level of interest rates. Your scenario would then be a combination of an interest rate level and a housing price level. Assume the price of the house after six months could have been $100,000 with a probability of 60 percent, $120,000 with a probability of 30 percent, and $70,000 with a probability of 20 percent. You would then have nine scenarios—all possible combinations of interest rate levels and house price levels, as shown in Figure 7.3. The first scenario has a house price of $70,000 coupled with an interest rate of 5 percent at the end of six months. The second scenario has a house price of $70,000 coupled with an interest rate of 10 percent at the end of six months; and so on. The last scenario has a house price of $120,000 coupled with an interest rate of 5 percent at the end of six months.

Any amount of complexity is possible. The important point is that the analysis remains the same. There are always some scenarios with final values that are positive and others with ending values that are negative. Without that variation, the scenarios would not reflect the full range of possible outcomes. After these values have been calculated, we can reduce the problem to an Upside and a downside. We value the Upside and downside separately and compute a risk-adjusted value. If it is positive, the deal makes economic sense.

Although these examples might seem simplistic, they are very close to real-world situations in which, if risk-adjusted valuation had been used, some extremely large firms would not have faded or disappeared. A telling case is Apple Computer. Think how different its

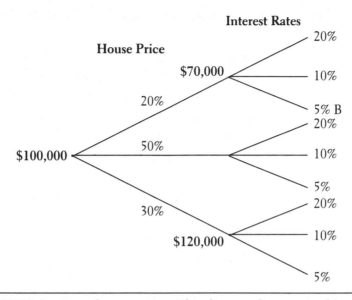

FIGURE 7.3 **Complex scenarios.** This diagram shows a combination of housing prices (three scenarios: $70,000, $100,000, and $120,000) and interest rates (also three scenarios: 20 percent, 10 percent, and 5 percent). Point B occurs, for example, when a $70,000 purchase price coincides with a 5 percent interest rate.

fortunes might have been if it had worked with firms that wished to "clone" its machines. Instead, since the mid-1980s, it has suffered a protracted decline, overtaken by less user-friendly but more commercially savvy rivals.

EVA Evangelists

Another instance where a Marking-to-Future approach offers insight involves the longstanding problem of measuring how well a firm's managers are performing. With help from a lot of highly paid management consultants, this has become a major issue. Given how generously many chief executives and chairpersons are rewarded these days, perhaps this is not surprising. But it is curious that such a simple problem has generated so much hot air.

Some of that warm draft has been felt by Siemens, a German high-tech manufacturing firm. In October 1997, it formally embraced a measurement fad known as Economic Value Added (EVA), thereby joining a group of international pioneers that includes Coca-Cola, Procter & Gamble, and Monsanto. EVA is one of several popular "performance metrics," as management consultants call them. The idea is easily stated: measure how much value a firm has created or destroyed. But putting the idea into practice is devilishly difficult.

On the surface, the principles behind EVA seem sensible enough. They start with investors' need for a benchmark. Assume a company is using $1 billion of capital to fund its operations and factories. Investors in the company's shares can only judge how well they are doing by comparing their returns from dividends and capital gains with the returns they might have earned from an alternative investment. In other words, they could have parceled out their money somewhere else and, for a similar amount of risk, earned more. EVA extends this overall measure of performance to everything a firm does.

For example, EVA deducts from a firm's net operating profits a charge for the amount of capital it has used. If the result is positive, the firm is deemed to have created "value"; if negative, the firm is tarred as a "value destroyer." (Presumably, its managers then hang their heads in shame and voluntarily give up their stock options!) If a firm can calculate a capital charge for each of its operating units, it can also assign them an EVA number. Thus, a division that, in one year, uses $100 million of capital at a cost of 10 percent will have to make a return of more than 10 percent if it is to generate a positive EVA. If it earns $50 million that year, its EVA will be $40 million.

That sounds simple, but real-life EVA calculations get more complicated because firms' published accounts have to be revised before any meaningful numbers can be crunched. Table 7.8 shows how

TABLE 7.8
EVA: South African Breweries Forecast Balance Sheet

Measures of Returns	Rand (in millions)
1. Economic capital =	
Shareholder's equity	5,799
+ goodwill written off	1,521
+ capitalized cumulative unusual loss	930
+ deferred tax	405
+ minority interests	2,352
+ total debt	4,415
	15,422
2. Net operating profit after tax (NOPAT) =	
Operating profit	4,306
+ interest expense	689
− unusual gain	68
− taxes	978
	3,049
3. Weighted average cost of capital (WACC)	
Cost of equity	20.4%
Cost of debt	10.7%
WACC =	17.5%
4. EVA = NOPAT − (capital × WACC)	
= 3,049 − (15,422 × 17.5%) =	350

Source: *The Economist.*

South African Breweries measures up under EVA. Let's examine how these results were calculated. The method for this belongs to Stern Stewart, a leading consulting firm that has registered EVA as a trademark in several countries and has gone so far as to register the term "EVAngelist."

The first step is to measure the firm's "economic capital"—the amount of capital it is using directly or indirectly, including sums that have been spent in the expectation that they will earn money in the future. Then the firm's after-tax profits are totaled up. The third step is to work out the cost of the firm's capital. Its debt costs are easy enough; the average rate of interest on its overall debt gives a useful figure. But how is its cost of equity calculated? Stern Stewart uses modern finance theory to assign a cost. In simple terms, how risky are a firm's shares relative to the market in which they trade? If they are a lot riskier, then the cost of equity is correspondingly higher. South African Breweries' cost of equity comes out at 20.4 percent. The weighted average of the cost of its equity and debt capital turns out to be 17.5 percent. The final step is to run the EVA formula. On this basis, South African Breweries should have a satisfied bunch of shareholders. It produced 350 million rand of EVA in 1996.

We have taken the trouble to explain EVA because we think it is symptomatic of the risk management problems that we are trying to solve. The underlying point of EVA is to measure how well or how badly a firm's managers have performed. The shareholders, the firm's owners, have appointed the managers to be guardians of the firm's assets. The owners want to be sure that these guardians have made good decisions on their behalf and have invested wisely. The guardians want to do their best because they stand to get rewarded—first, by keeping their jobs, and second, by meeting performance-related bonus targets. Does EVA indicate whether the managers have done well? Perhaps more to the point, does it give any idea of how well the managers will do in future?

These are telling questions. In *The Economist*, an article about EVA pointed out one problem: EVA is backward-looking; it fails to tell owners and guardians "how their current strategies are likely to affect the future value of their companies." EVA gives little indication of looming problems. For instance, Robert Citron, the infamous treasurer of Orange County, produced twelve years' worth of superb EVA. But a single bad year cost him his job and lost the county a fortune. EVA has severe limitations as a risk-adjusted way of viewing decisions.

There is also a fundamental problem with a central step in EVA. When the cost of capital is measured, it locks in a view of managers' performance that tells very little about their skill. In effect, the cost of capital number that is generated today becomes a single scenario for measuring past performance or for evaluating a deal tomorrow. Under that scenario, a firm's managers might decide not to invest in a new factory because the projected EVA looked inadequate. But they might make an alternative investment. Indeed, let's assume for a moment that they made a risk-adjusted decision of the kind we have advocated. The decision is unlucky and the deal goes sour. If the managers use EVA, the firm's owners might be shocked; their guardians' performance would look terrible. But did the guardians really make a bad decision? No. They weighed the Upside and their potential Regret and judged the deal worth doing, given their risk profile.

Let's look again at the calculation of the cost of capital. Does it really make sense to base the firm's debt costs on its average interest rate today? If a portion of its debt is set at floating interest rates, then its true costs could fluctuate wildly, especially if it is operating in volatile economies that are subject to big swings in rates. Looking forward, there might be scenarios under which the real cost of debt could range from 12 percent to 25 percent. If this variability were taken into account, then the firm's EVA numbers would change dramatically. Consider, in the example in Table 7.8, the tremendous volatility in South African interest rates and the uncertainty surrounding these rates because of the political scene in that country.

We think the problem with EVA, and with other measures that track corporate managers' performance, is similar to the mutual fund issue we described at the start of this chapter. Instead of marking values to market and producing a single calculation today, we should mark values to tomorrow—marking-to-future, as we call it. Using a tree diagram, most deals and decisions can be marked to future. Managers and investors alike can then make proper risk-adjusted calculations.

We can illustrate this point in a simple but powerful way. Using the numbers shown in Table 7.8 for South African Breweries, imagine another company called South African Breweries II (SAB II). In 1996, SAB II produced 350 million rand of EVA. If you were an investor, you might be sufficiently impressed to buy its shares. But you would be making a huge mistake.

The reason is that, unbeknown to you, SAB II has been the beneficiary of something done by a clever manager fourteen years ago. He saw an opportunity to make a huge bond issue when interest rates were very low. Ever since, the company has had a very low average cost of debt. But the bond issue is about to mature. SAB II will have to refinance in today's much higher interest-rate environment. Moreover, there is a danger that interest rates in South Africa might shoot up in the event of some political calamity. What could happen to SAB II's EVA?

Here are two simple scenarios. Assume current interest rates in South Africa are 15.6 percent. In the first scenario, things are rosy and interest rates a year hence will have fallen only slightly, to 14 percent. This lowers both debt and equity costs and is great news for SAB II. It is able to refinance its debt efficiently, so its weighted cost of capital (WACC) falls to 16.9 percent. As Table 7.9 shows, under this scenario, SAB II's EVA rises to 443 million rand, a healthy gain over the year just past.

In the second scenario, however, South Africa suffers a major economic setback. Rates rise to 25 percent, and even after its best efforts at refinancing, SAB II finds that its WACC jumps to 21 percent. Now look at its EVA (Table 7.10); it has not so much collapsed as disappeared. Under this scenario, SAB II will destroy value worth 189 million rand.

Let's analyze these results using Upside and Regret. Assume we think there is a 70 percent chance that the benign (first) scenario will occur. Our decision tree will be as shown in Figure 7.4.

Our Upside is easy enough to calculate—it is a 93 million rand increase over 350 million rand. But look at our Regret—an enormous 539 million rand! We might conclude that SAB II faces a big risk in the

TABLE 7.9
*EVA: South African Breweries Balance Sheet under Scenario I**

	Measures of Returns	Rand (in millions)
1.	Economic capital =	
	Shareholder's equity	5,799
	+ goodwill written off	1,521
	+ capitalized cumulative unusual loss	930
	+ deferred tax	405
	+ minority interests	2,352
	+ total debt	4,415
		15,422
2.	Net operating profit after tax (NOPAT) =	
	Operating profit	4,306
	+ interest expense	689
	− unusual gain	68
	− taxes	978
		3,049
3.	Weighted average cost of capital (WACC)	
	Cost of equity	19.2%
	Cost of debt	10.1%
	WACC =	16.9%
4.	EVA = NOPAT − (capital × WACC)	
	= 3,049 − (15,422 × 16.9%) =	443

* Interest rates are at 14 percent.

future, thanks mainly to the structure of its balance sheet. If interest rates rise sharply, it will suffer a serious drop in performance that will have little to do with the operating skills of its managers. In fact, those managers might consult our framework to ask themselves whether they should in`sure against the downside risk, perhaps by buying options that will pay off in the event of a big rise in interest rates. As for investors, a

TABLE 7.10
EVA: South African Breweries Balance Sheet under
*Scenario II**

Measures of Returns	Rand (in millions)
1. Economic capital =	
Shareholder's equity	5,799
+ goodwill written off	1,521
+ capitalized cumulative unusual loss	930
+ deferred tax	405
+ minority interests	2,352
+ total debt	4,415
	15,422
2. Net operating profit after tax (NOPAT) =	
Operating profit	4,306
+ interest expense	689
− unusual gain	68
− taxes	978
	3,049
3. Weighted average cost of capital (WACC)	
Cost of equity	23.0%
Cost of debt	15.0%
WACC =	21.0%
4. EVA = NOPAT − (capital × WACC)	
= 3,049 − (15,422 × 21.0%) =	−189

* Interest rates rise to 25 percent.

risk-adjusted forward-looking view of the firm might put off all but the most optimistic.

Our example is obviously simplified. We have made several assumptions about the effects of altered rates on SAB II's finances, and we have used only two scenarios. But the central point is that EVA tells us little or nothing about the future risks faced by this firm, just as total

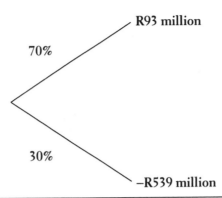

R93 million

70%

30%

−R539 million

FIGURE 7.4 **Mark-to-future for South African Breweries's Economic Value Added (EVA).** The EVA today is 350 million rand. It could go up to 443, giving an Upside of 93, or it could go down to − 189, giving a total Downside of 539 (350 + 189).

past returns give us no indication of how a mutual fund will perform next year. These are narrow snapshots. We need a panoramic view that includes what might happen tomorrow. Put another way, we need to take a forward-looking view, "Marking EVA-to-Future," and to compute a risk-adjusted EVA (REVA).

Chapter 8

OF LIFE, LOTTERIES, AND STOCK OPTIONS

When one of the authors was a naive college student, he sat drinking coffee with friends one lazy afternoon and encountered an age-old excitement. One of his group remarked that he had just done a clever thing. In response to a chain letter, he had sent a total of about $75 to four people named in the letter. In return, his name would be featured on the recipient list as the chain continued, and it would rise to the top after the letter was passed along a few times. At that point, he would suddenly be flooded with money worth his $75 many times over. Half of the group's reaction was to laugh. How could our friend have been so silly? Didn't he know that he was unlikely ever to see a penny because these schemes do the rounds occasionally and rarely benefit more than a tiny number of people? That $75 could have been better used buying a few rounds of drinks in the college bar.

But the other half of the group was intrigued, and an earnest, if somewhat greedy, discussion ensued. If this letter had proved so compelling that one of us had actually sent off money, surely there was gold in the links of the chain. All we had to do was to start our own letter, thereby ensuring that the early returns would reach us before the project ran out of steam. Alas, it was not so simple, as we soon discovered. None of us—including the friend who originally captured our interest—ever saw a penny of return on the idea, but several weeks of effort and hope were spent in vain before we learned the truth about Ponzi schemes.

Why do such schemes trap so many, and why are they so persistent? The question is important because pyramid investment schemes have been plaguing some countries' efforts to emerge from communist rule. Romania endured a couple of fantastic schemes in the mid-1990s — schemes that temporarily offered people a quick escape from poverty, but ruined those who were trapped when the party stopped. In Albania, crooked investment schemes were directly implicated in the breakdown of civil order in 1997. So many people had invested in the schemes that the social pain was intolerable when they collapsed. Even when they knew that the schemes were incredibly risky, people went on investing their money, hoping that they would get out before the last and final round.

Ponzi schemes work because they cleverly appeal to our sense of Upside. They create a false view of positive risk-adjusted return by exaggerating the Upside relative to a small, fixed downside. Poor college students and Albanians probably shared the hope that if only they could grasp the promised returns, their lives would be greatly improved. The loss of $75, though painful, would not be disastrous for most students. But when thousands of people lost everything in Albania, their Regret was so high that they took to the streets. It is reckoned that as much as $2 billion was lost in Albania's pyramid schemes, equivalent to around half that country's official gross annual economic output.

Pyramid schemes are not limited to cash rip-offs; they come in many guises. How many of us know friends or family who have been seduced, even if temporarily, into buying expensive stocks of vitamin pills, vacuum cleaners, or cosmetics? The promise is always a variation on the theme that this wonder product, which is usually not available in retail shops, will yield wealth and prosperity. A few people, through perseverance and previously latent sales ability, do work their way to the top of the heap. But the common thread in all of these schemes is that almost all of the benefits accrue to those who initiate and run them. Those lower on the chain are usually working to enrich those at the top. They do it because they put a high weight on the Upside. In noncash schemes, the Upside might not be represented by purely monetary concerns. For instance, some people undoubtedly are attracted to pyramid selling schemes because they yearn for the imagined independence of "working for myself." These people value a psychological Upside more than the financial Regret caused by owning more shampoo than they can ever use.

If pyramid schemes were properly analyzed by their potential victims, most would simply fail. The same should be true of the many lotteries that offer poor chances of success. The risk-adjusted valuation approach we have developed is a good way to understand why we play lotteries even when the odds are overwhelmingly against us (Figure 8.1).

As we write this book, a Toronto lottery is selling tickets for $100, on a prize of $1 million. By law, the total number of available tickets must be announced in the press. In this case, it is 30,000. Assuming the lottery promoter sells all the tickets, there is a one in 30,000

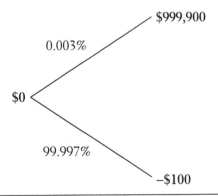

FIGURE 8.1 Scenario diagram for a Toronto lottery. This diagram depicts the process of valuing a decision to buy a lottery ticket advertised in a Toronto newspaper. The ticket costs $100 and has a prize of $1 million. The net gain is therefore, $999,900. The chances of winning are one in 30,000 or 0.003 percent. Consequently, the chances of losing are 99.997 percent and the amount we can lose is in the price of the ticket.

chance of winning. Thus, the fair or expected value of the ticket should be 1/30,000th of a million dollars, or $33. Yet the lottery is greatly over-subscribed, and many mathematicians, teachers, and university profes-sors are among those who are buying tickets! Lotteries have been famously described as a "tax on the stupid." How do we explain the fact that, in this case, PhDs are among the apparently gullible? The answer comes from analyzing the example using our risk-adjusted approach.

When we use scenario trees to describe the lottery, we see that the downside is $100 (the cost of the ticket) and the upside is $999,900 (the net amount the winner will earn from the lottery, $1,000,000 – $100). We now break the problem into two decisions: a bet (Figure 8.2) and in-surance (Figure 8.3).

For the bet (the Upside), we ask you what is the most you would pay for a very, very small chance of winning almost a million dollars (Figure 8.2). Many people would pay more than $100 for such an opportunity.

For the insurance (the downside), we ask: How much would you spend to insure an almost certain loss of $100 (Figure 8.3)? The amount would be some number less than $100. (You can only lose $100, so why spend $100 or more on insuring the loss?)

The risk-adjusted value would then be positive (more than $100 minus some number less than $100, which is positive). Therefore, we expect people to play the lottery. Participants are not as stupid as they might seem!

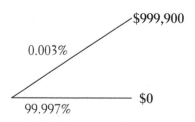

FIGURE 8.2   Toronto lottery. The Upside is $1 million minus the cost of the ticket.

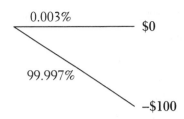

FIGURE 8.3   Toronto lottery. The Downside is precisely the cost of the ticket.

The difference between the lottery and the pyramid schemes is that sometimes, particularly when the payoffs are large, people will be prepared to pay much more than the expected value for a bet. In this case, they pay $100—far more than the expected value, which is $33.

Another interesting aspect of human behavior in such decisions is what happens when the amounts are changed but the odds aren't. For example, what if the Toronto lottery had the same odds (1 in 30,000) but read "A chance to win $1 billion" (1,000 times more) and the tickets cost $100,000 (also 1,000 times more). There would be far fewer takers for this lottery. Why? Because the loss of $100,000 with near certainty would be devastating to many, and this loss would dominate their thinking. The Regret in this case is too high.

Another way of expressing this decision is: We would pay more to insure an almost certain loss of $100,000 (downside insurance) than we would pay for a very small chance of winning a billion dollars (Upside value). Very few people would even be able to contemplate spending $33,333 (the expected value)—never mind $100,000 (the scaled-up ticket price)—for a ticket that has a very small chance of winning, no matter how great the possible reward. Yet, for the scaled-down lottery, people were prepared to pay more than the expected value of the bet. As the stakes get very high, the value of the downside outweighs the value of the Upside, and the risk-adjusted value is negative.

In many circumstances, investment or other choices involving financial uncertainty would involve more than a simple choice between

Upside and downside. There will be many possible scenarios and, hence, many possible outcomes. But at the end of the day, all financial decision problems, as well as many nonfinancial ones, can be reduced to the risk-adjusted analysis we have demonstrated.

For each decision we have to make, there is an Upside and a downside. When the market is incomplete, the values associated with the Upside and downside will be subjective. These values determine how the decision maker discounts future earnings or losses under the Upside and downside scenarios. To see this, let's look again at the example we studied in Chapter 3. Recall that you have received a $3,000 gift. Your broker offers to invest it in a fund and outlines the possibilities as follows. After one month, the $3,000 will increase to $4,000 with a likelihood of 80 percent, or it will be worth zero with 20 percent likelihood (Figure 8.4).

Because the future value is $1,000 for the Upside and today's value, as given by the decision maker, is $300, we can deduce that the discount factor applied to the upside is $^{300}/_{1,000}$ or $^{3}/_{10}$. In a similar fashion, we can say that the decision maker has discounted the downside value in the future to get today's value of $^{100}/_{3,000}$ or $^{1}/_{30}$.

These discount factors are extremely useful if we wish to obtain a risk-adjusted value for a similar problem with future payoffs that are not far different from the ones above. For example, we might ask what the risk-adjusted value would be if the downside future loss was $3,900 and the Upside future value was only $500. The downside value would be $^{1}/_{30}$ of $3,900, which equals $130. The Upside value would be $^{3}/_{10}$ of $500, which equals $150. The risk-adjusted value would then be $20.

Even more interesting is the view this decision maker has implied by the valuation given. The "implied view" is the set of probabilities and the discount rate that we can determine from valuation of the Upside and downside. In this case, the discount factors are $^{3}/_{10}$ ($= ^{9}/_{30}$) and $^{1}/_{30}$, respectively. Thus, the implied view is a probability of $^{9}/_{10}$ for the Upside and $^{1}/_{10}$ for the downside, and a discount rate of $^{1}/_{3}$ for the period. Note that $(^{1}/_{3}) \times (^{9}/_{10}) = ^{9}/_{30} = ^{3}/_{10}$ and $(^{1}/_{3}) \times (^{1}/_{10}) = ^{1}/_{30}$. These are the discount factors implied by the decision maker.

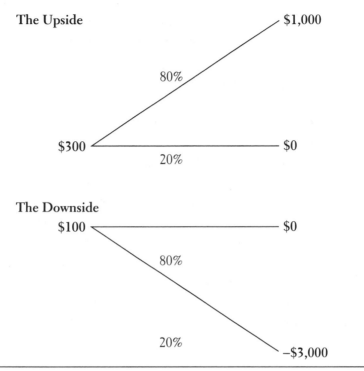

FIGURE 8.4 Investing $3,000—the Upside and the Downside. The Upside is what we would pay for the bet to win $1,000. The Downside is what we would pay to insure against the loss of $3,000.

We can interpret this in the following way. The decision maker has associated an implied probability of 9/10 with the Upside event, which exceeds the objective probability that was associated with the Upside. The implied view is that the Upside should be weighted more heavily than indicated and, consequently, the downside should be discounted relative to the expected value. Another way of expressing this is to say that the implied view is "bullish."

This simple observation has enormous implications. For instance, with this limited information, we can learn a great deal about a decision maker and then tailor contracts that are highly likely to be appealing. This significantly enhances our negotiating position. At the very least, it means that we can set a range of values beyond which we know that our potential counterparty will not be interested in dealing with us.

This knowledge has tremendous potential value for negotiators. At present, we go through lengthy games as we try to sound out a would-be counterparty or customer. It can be very hard to read people's intentions because we have no way of knowing what they are really thinking. Will they offer a low price? If so, what would this signal? Is it really an opening bid, or are they serious about walking away if the price is higher? Should we demand a very high price at the outset and be prepared to reduce it later? Or should we pitch a realistic price? A standard rule is that we should always try to avoid making the first offer because we immediately give our opponent an advantage by signaling our base case. Or should we try to influence the risk-adjusted value by suggesting some "scare" scenarios?

This is where implied views can help. In a situation where we are selling something and have six possible buyers, we might ask them to submit preliminary bids based on identical information. We might then ask them to tell us, under various scenarios, what they would be prepared to bid. Provided we have framed the bidding request correctly, we might find that we can eliminate four parties simply by taking their bids and calculating their implied views, which reveal that they are significantly less bullish than the remaining two. In other words, we would know that these potential buyers are far less likely to bid the highest price for what we are selling. We can narrow our efforts to the most bullish buyers—those who are likely to see the highest risk-adjusted value in our product or property. And we can negotiate from a position of relative strength because we are fairly confident that our bullish buyers want to do a deal—they can see positive value in the trade.

There is nothing stopping buyers from also using this technique. For instance, they could canvass possible suppliers with a request for information about prices and quantities under certain scenarios. Using the information provided, they could calculate the suppliers' implied views and focus their efforts on the two that seem likeliest to want to do a deal.

Options, Options

The fact that someone's implied views can be bullish (or bearish) also lends a clue as to why the combination of Upside and Regret is a better way of describing people's behavior than that provided by classical economics. In Chapter 4, we met Microsoft Man. His implied view was bullish in the extreme. He thought Microsoft shares were a one-way bet, so he underweighted Regret and overconcentrated his portfolio. Provided he could afford large losses in the event that Microsoft shares were to fall, his behavior was not necessarily irrational. Microsoft Man has plenty of company, not least among Microsoft employees. Many of them have become extremely rich, thanks to the firm's generous attitude toward stock options.

Options have become a standard means for corporations to reward employees because they appear to offer a genuine *win–win* contract—that is, one in which both sides to a deal think they have a positive risk-adjusted value. To traditional economists, this appears puzzling. Aren't deals that are properly priced necessarily win–lose contracts? Wouldn't someone who is thinking of granting stock options do so only if the options seemed to be properly priced? On the other side, employees must often forgo salary in order to receive options—something they would be reluctant to do if they thought the options were overpriced. In isolation, based on each side's expected values, it is hard to see how in a world of symmetric contracts there would be any stock options. The two sides simply could not arrive at a mutually agreeable price.

The solution to this conundrum is that options can represent win–win contracts in certain circumstances. If we put Upside and Regret into the equation, it is easy to see that, for both sides, stock options offer significant Upside, offset by little Regret. For the entrepreneur, options can defer salary costs during a period when the firm desperately needs its cash flow. Alternatively, options can be a way of holding on to valuable staff whom the firm could not otherwise afford to keep. Imagine that a key staff member at a small but fast-growing technology firm is offered a fat salary by an established rival. The small firm cannot possibly match the salary offer, not least because it could not afford to set such a precedent among its remaining workers. But it can use options (future returns) as a way of enticing the employee to stay. In effect, the entrepreneur dangles Upside to employees whose implied views are sufficiently bullish that they see a positive risk-adjusted value. An employee who still chose to leave could incur a great deal of Regret if it turned out that the firm was floated on the stock market and went on to perform spectacularly.

This is no abstract problem; these events happen every day. Small firms are usually particularly vulnerable to the demands of a small number of their top employees. Typically, these managers dominate the firm's external contacts; they represent it at sales meetings and trade conferences and consequently come to the attention of rivals that are always looking for talent. It is common for well-established firms to pitch lucrative offers. If you are currently being paid $60,000 and a few options, and a big firm offers you $400,000 and a guaranteed bonus of $100,000 after one year, you would be a rare person if you were not seriously tempted. But if your firm's options are potentially worth $2 million and the firm might float them in a year's time, then the temptation to leave will be dramatically smaller.

When a firm is no longer fast-growing, options can become a less attractive form of reward. At Microsoft, for instance, many of its young programmers (called "geeks") became fabulously wealthy because of their options. The firm's booming stock price meant that even relatively recent arrivals could accumulate significant wealth. This has left the firm vulnerable to its own staff. Instead of being beholden to the firm, plenty of staff have sufficient wealth that they can walk away any time they choose. Many have done so, opting to explore the slower-paced world of not-for-profit enterprises or to start the families that they deferred while writing code for Bill Gates.

A rise in the share price also has a paradoxical effect: it increases the now wealthy employees' potential Regret. If you own a bunch of options, which have not vested, then your Upside is largely theoretical until the moment you can cash them in. But once your options have vested, then you have a real exposure to the firm. Should its share price suddenly collapse, you will experience massive Regret. This is what many Microsoft employees have in common with Microsoft Man: having enjoyed the Upside, they now face large Regret because their wealth is very concentrated. Indeed, in some ways, the company encourages this. Employees can opt for a number of pension and savings plans that allow them to buy Microsoft shares at a discount. Many staff choose to "save" as much as they can this way. Historically, such offerings have been extremely lucrative.

Microsoft's spectacular success has meant that its new employees no longer find options as alluring as their predecessors did. As Microsoft has grown, it has increasingly taken on staff who do not fit into the geek category. Indeed, thanks to the firm's efforts in an array of businesses, it now has many staff who barely know their way around a PC. These staff approach share options from a new angle. Is it likely, for instance, that the firm's shares will experience the same Upside in the next five years as in the past five years? Almost certainly not—in which case, options will prove a significantly less attractive alternative to salary. Many new Microsoft employees are people in the middle of their careers, and they live in cities such as New York, where it costs real money to rent apartments and buy dinner. In theory, they might like to forgo some salary in favor of options. But in practice, their immediate need for cash precludes them from exposure to the Upside. That situation can create curious resentments. For instance, a newly appointed senior manager might feel quite peculiar when confronted by a much younger subordinate who happens to be a multimillionaire.

It is hard to overstate the obsession with options among businesses and workers alike. In America, options have become a standard tool in corporate finance. It is reckoned that, among America's top 200 firms, options now account for nearly 12 percent of shares outstanding, compared with less than 7 percent at the end of the 1980s. In the mid-1980s, the value of shares set aside for options was around $60 billion. These days, the number is more like $300 billion. (As we write this book, stock markets are hovering around their highest-ever levels. By the time you read this book, however, they might not be so elevated.)

Fashion-conscious firms abroad have jumped on the bandwagon. One only has to see the fuss over the options-laden pay packets of bosses of privatized water and electrical utilities in Britain to see how far the game has gone. But it is a dangerous game on all sides. Inherent in it is a single scenario: the share price will rise sufficiently that the options will have value. The benefits to the firm last until options have vested. The benefits to the employee accrue only after options have vested, but then serve to decouple the employee's interests from those of the firm.

Some firms have long been aware of the pros and cons of options. Investment banks, for example, are plagued by an options-related problem. At each year-end, they award their staff bonuses based on performance during that year. These payouts are the equivalent of options vesting; during the year, staff in effect have a call option on the firm's Upside. The problem for banks is that, once bonuses have been paid, the staff have no incentive to stay if a rival makes a higher bid for their skills. No sooner do bankers cash in then many of them check out. Moreover, bonus schemes have caused perverse behavior. Banks come under great pressure to pay bonuses, even when they have not had particularly profitable years. They argue that this is the only way to keep their best people, just as other firms claim that stock options are the only way to keep theirs. In addition, banks have to make sure that their traders are not taking undue risks as they chase the high returns that will bring them life-altering bonuses. In other words, traders should be encouraged to pursue the Upside, but the firm should make sure that they are not exposing it to Regret. Every deal the bank enters into should make sense on a risk-adjusted basis!

Many investment banks have taken steps to resolve this option-related problem. They now withhold a chunk of their staff's bonuses for a set period—sometimes a year or two, sometimes longer. Instead of being paid all in cash, a portion of bonuses is now paid in the form of shares, with the intent to tie workers to the firm. Anyone who leaves for a rival firm is forced to give up any bonus entitlements. There can be an occasional opposite effect, as one or two banks have found. Deferred compensation can make it more difficult to winkle out employees whose departure would cause no Regret!

Other firms are learning, too, that options can have a dark side. In several firms in the United States, shareholders have revolted after managers voted themselves particularly generous options. And during 1997, there was the beginning of a widespread realization that if options are too rich for managers, then the firm can actually suffer harm. If a group of determined managers wished, they could effectively manage the firm to maximize share prices up to the point where options would become hugely valuable. One academic study found that managers who have big dollops of options tend to be keener to make "strategic" acquisitions and divestitures, as if to justify to shareholders that they are working for their rewards. Another study found that an embarrassing number of firms award stock options to managers just before the firm reports a spree of good news that sends its stock price soaring. In such cases, options cease to be win–win contracts; rather, they become instruments by which managers grab value from shareholders.

In response, the best-managed firms are tempering their use of options. In Chapter 7, we mentioned that Monsanto is among those firms

that have embraced EVA. It is also a pioneer of stock options for bosses
that offer win–win terms to shareholders. Its managers are rewarded in
two ways. First, four sets of options are triggered as and when the share
price passes set levels of $150, $175, $200, and $225, against a current
share price of around $40. Second, and innovatively, managers are re-
quired to purchase shares in Monsanto using money that the company
lends to them. Only if they meet some stiff targets—performing better
than three-quarters of a group of industrial rivals for a set number of
years, for instance—do they keep the shares. Otherwise, they must use
their own money to pay the company back. Announcing the new structure, Monsanto's chairman said that he and his colleagues would be
subject to "both the upward opportunities and the downside risks inherent in stock ownership." (Again, it is interesting how often people
use Upside and Regret without knowing that they are doing so. In this
case, the chairman might have noted that the scheme was intended to
ensure that managers share Regret with shareholders—something that
will naturally give them similar incentives.)

Heads You Win, Tails I Lose

In general, then, stock options are an example of a win–win contract. In
defiance of conventional finance theory, both parties to the contract are
happy because they calculate the risk-adjusted value of the options
differently and can therefore agree on a price. Financial, business/
commercial, and even sporting life is full of examples of such contracts.
Consider the following evidence:

- Swaps. Both sides benefit from these financial transactions,
  which convert interest payments either from fixed to floating
  rates (or vice versa) or from one currency into another. In a typical currency swap, for instance, a U.S. firm that can borrow

cheaply in its home market converts the money to a foreign currency, say French francs, by swapping with a French firm that wishes to borrow in dollars. Both firms end up with cheaper funds than they could have raised on their own.

- Catastrophe insurance bonds such as the hurricane bonds described in Chapter 2.

- Credit derivatives. These are new instruments that allow banks to pass along concentrations in their lending caused by accidents of geography. For instance, an American bank might pass along some of its credit risk to its local borrowers in return for taking on some of the credit risk of an Italian bank. The chances that both types of borrowers will default at the same time are obviously much lower than the chance that one set of borrowers will run into trouble.

- Michael Jordan's multimillion-dollar contract with the Chicago Bulls (so long as he goes on shooting hoops better than anyone else).

- Tiger Woods's lucrative endorsement contract with Nike (ditto, but substitute golf balls for hoops).

- Credit card loyalty programs. Whatever the card issuer gives up by way of rewards, it gains from increased contact with its customers over time.

- Savings plans offered by telephone companies. As competition has heated up in America and other countries, phone companies have offered consumers a savings bonanza. For instance, an AT&T customer in New York switched his long-distance business to MCI's 12-cents-a-minute plan, only to be offered $50 to switch back to AT&T's "new" 12-cents-a-minute plan. Despite sharply reduced revenues from calls, AT&T still benefits because it profits from line rentals and other services. Hence its newfound willingness to offer a winning deal to consumers!

Many consumers' long-distance phone bills have been reduced by four-fifths in the past two or three years.

- Mutual and cooperative societies. These work when members collectively can do business more efficiently than if they acted as individuals. For instance, a mutually owned mortgage company can use the power of numbers to offer its members cheaper home loans. Society membership offers a win–win contract.

Where people or firms fail to make proper risk-adjusted calculations, they might still find themselves in win–lose contracts. The most glaring example of a firm shot through with such contracts is Britain's Barings Bank. When it collapsed in early 1995, most people drew a single lesson: a rogue trader had been allowed, through a combination of incompetence and greed, to run up losses that literally broke the bank. Thinking of the episode in terms of Upside and downside creates a much more nuanced picture of the Barings downfall. For instance, Nicholas Leeson (the rogue trader) had a free option on the Upside and very little personal Regret until his crimes got out of hand. For him, the operational and trading freedoms he was allowed amounted to a contract in which he would gain, at the bank's expense. He stood to make big bonuses so long as his trading schemes continued and he was reporting substantial profits to London.

There, his bosses were seduced by the impact his profits would have on their own bonuses. They mistakenly saw his profits as resulting from a win–win contract. Because of the optionlike nature of the bank's bonus schemes, those managers were concerned for their own Upside, and thus largely failed to protect the firm as a whole (and its bondholders, who thought their investment was ironclad) from Regret. Their implied view was wholeheartedly bullish, which makes it less amazing, with hindsight, that there was very little interrogation of Leeson's profits before it was too late. For the bank to be making such huge profits in Singapore, was it not taking risk or committing fraud? If the bank had adjusted Leeson's performance for those risks, it would have formed a very different picture of his behavior long before he had run up huge losses. In the wake of Leeson's antics, many banks now have a healthy suspicion of Upside that appears unusually strong: Where did these returns come from and how much risk was taken in order to earn them? Even where a bank is bullish and therefore inclined to seek risk, it has become far more common to question success as well as failure.

Another sad example of a win–lose contract is the experience of Sony Corporation in Hollywood. It signed up leading studio executives with what looked like win–win contracts. It failed to realize, however, that it had, in effect, handed those executives a blank check with which to spend its shareholders' money. When Sony bought into Hollywood, it saw mainly the Upside of one big box office hit after another. It underplayed the downside risk represented by a string of expensive flops, which is precisely what happened. If it had adopted a risk-adjusted stance, it might have structured its contracts more sensibly—only rewarding managers if they delivered results, and putting clear limits on the managers' ability to spend money. Any firm, upon hearing that a subsidiary has a reputation for lavish spending, especially in an industry that is hard to impress, should pay serious attention. The chances are that it is suffering from a win–lose contract that will cause it Regret.

A remarkable win–lose contract was Michael Ovitz's infamous $97 million reward in 1977, after only nine months with Disney. Ovitz is a talented entertainment executive, but it seems crazy that he or any other individual can ever earn so much money for so little work. The losers on the contract were Disney shareholders, who got little if anything for a large expenditure. In general, when managers are granted "golden egg" clauses in their contracts, it is at shareholders' expense. The managers in question rarely have a deserving case for so much Upside, even if they manage to persuade a board of directors that the opposite is true. Indeed, the fact that a potential recruit even asks for a golden egg might be seen as implying a bearish view regarding his or her prospects.

Another common win–lose contract is the subject of enormous vexation and remarkable passivity. The parties involved usually know from experience that they are entering into a horribly skewed deal, but they go ahead and do it anyway: they contract to buy a house. The craziest case can be found in Britain—specifically, in England. House buyers there have amazingly little power, except in one circumstance when they can turn the tables on sellers. Assume for a moment that house prices are rising and you wish to buy. A seller asks for £200,000 and you are willing to pay that price. You agree to a deal and shake hands. Under the English system, however, it can take several weeks before formal and legally binding contracts are "exchanged." And in this period, a terrible thing can happen. Known as "gazumping," essentially the seller exercises a free option to sell at a higher price to someone else. It is unclear whether the nastiest form of gazumping is where the seller uses the threat to pull out as a means of extracting more money from the original purchaser, or where the seller simply pulls out and deals with a new buyer. Whatever the sequence, enormous stress and misunderstanding are the results. The real estate agents who act as intermediaries in these deals have little incentive to arbitrate or seek fair play. In the end, their commission will be higher if the final price is higher.

Occasionally, buyers have the same power, but in reverse. When prices are falling and demand for houses is also falling, a buyer might try to drop the price at the last minute by threatening to walk away. When this happened in Britain in the early 1990s, a generation of bruised homeowners called for reform of the system. Now that house prices are rising again, however, the bruising is happening all over again.

We can see why this system is crazy, if we analyze it using Upside and Regret. In a rising market, the seller incurs no downside by using gazumping to extract a higher price. There is no legal recourse for the maltreated original buyer. In one sense, therefore, it is perfectly rational for the seller to play this cruel game. After all, an extra £10,000 or £20,000 can make a big difference. Only personal morals might stop someone from chasing this Upside as hard as possible.

From the buyer's perspective, until contracts have been exchanged and a legal obligation has been established, the system is inherently unattractive. No business would grant, to a supplier or customer, a free option equivalent to the option that house buyers are forced to grant sellers. After all, the price of this option can turn out to be extremely high; in some cases, it can cost the buyer thousands of additional pounds. Alternatively, it can literally break a deal by moving the price beyond the buyer's means. The potential Regret is therefore enormous.

Why do people tolerate this system? The question is bizarre, because almost everyone in England either has firsthand experience of gazumping or has watched friends go through trauma as they played and got hurt in the housing market. One answer is that rising house prices are seen as conferring more net benefit than loss, so politicians have been reluctant to intervene. However, simple changes would remove the option that turns even the most honest sellers into potential deal breakers. In Scotland, for instance, there is no waiting period before a legal contract exists. Pulling out of deals there can involve forfeiting a deposit of up to 10 percent of the purchase price, something that concentrates the minds and morals of all parties. Indeed, by requiring both sides to make a deposit that can be forfeited, the Scottish system in effect places a premium on the option to walk away. Deals still fall through, of course, for reasons other than greed. In these cases, however, the deposits act as an insurance premium that protects the other party from harm. Because there is a single price on the option, Scottish buyers and sellers are treated the same. This is a win–win system, but those who practice it recognize that sometimes one party will lose.

England is not alone in its misery. Rising real estate prices in the United States often produce win–lose contracts, simply because housing demand tends to outstrip supply. In New York, for instance, bad habits became prevalent amid strong market conditions after mid-1996. Would-be buyers placed offers—and often mailed their deposit checks—only to find that theirs was one of several bids that the seller would keep on the table in case a rival deal fell through; until then, the seller had no intention of cashing their check. Horror stories abounded. In many cases, the reason for problems is the lack of a penalty affecting the seller. Although a 10 percent deposit is normally required from the buyer, the seller, in effect, keeps a free option on the Upside.

A Giant Sucking Sound

Britain offers one of the world's finest examples of a win–lose contract, an example that also powerfully illustrates how better thinking about risk can help us to avoid catastrophes. In 1992, executives at Hoover, a manufacturer of vacuum cleaners, came up with what they thought was a neat marketing ploy. Under pressure from Maytag, the American parent company, to improve sales and profits, Hoover's bosses endorsed a promotion that offered customers an attractive deal: if they spent £100 or more on a new Hoover product, they would earn two free round-trip air tickets to Europe. This proved successful—so much so that Hoover's factory began working around the clock to meet demand. Then, however, the firm's managers made a huge leap: far-away America became the promised destination for would-be purchasers. For the average traveler, such tickets were worth perhaps £400, far more than the value of the underlying product. Not surprisingly, sales of Hoovers more than jumped. Consumers by the thousand quickly realized that their Upside from the promotion was worth far more than the downside of buying a new machine that they may not have needed. Meanwhile, those who had thought of replacing an old or tired machine were given a powerful reason to buy a Hoover rather than a rival brand.

Promotions rely on the win–win idea if they are to be successful. Customers think they are getting a good deal, and the promoter achieves more sales than would otherwise have been gained. The extra costs for the promoter are thus offset by obvious benefits. Unfortunately, Hoover had blundered its way into a disastrous win–lose contract with its customers—and came out the loser. As more and more people claimed free air tickets, it became clear that the idea had gone much further than Hoover's management had ever anticipated. Rival businesses even began to exploit Hoover's embarrassment. One carpet retailer, for instance, cheekily offered a free Hoover to would-be customers for £999 or more worth of its carpet—a deal that explicitly carried with it the free air tickets promised by Hoover! As people bought new machines that they did not really need, they began to try to sell them for less than they had paid. After all, with air tickets in the bag, it scarcely mattered if a consumer "lost" £40 on a £100 purchase—the net result was £400 of air travel for a tenth of the price. A flourishing market in unused Hoover goods sprang up, cannibalizing the very business the promotion was supposed to help.

As the disaster unfolded, Maytag was forced to intervene. Three Hoover bosses were fired, including the highly-paid chief executive. In the end, Maytag had to set aside no less than £48 million to cover the fiasco. It set up a task force that, at its peak, had 250 staff trying to sort out the mess caused by tens of thousands of claims for tickets. By one estimate, some 100,000 Hoover products were purchased in 1992 and 1993, so the number of tickets at stake was huge. To top the commercial disaster, Hoover found itself with a customer relations nightmare. Thousands of people could not get the flights they expected, often because Hoover cited "small print" that limited availability. Many sued the firm, arguing that the promotion had been misleading. Lawsuits, some of which are still before the courts as we write, have cost Hoover further sums.

How could a company ever have contemplated such a promotion? On the face of it, Hoover never stood to make money on a deal that gave customers much more than they were paying to buy a vacuum cleaner. Indeed, a simple Upside–downside analysis would have been sufficient to alert Hoover's managers to their potential problem. But, like those corporate treasurers who bought exotic and risky derivatives because they had a big incentive to make small extra returns, Hoover's managers were under pressure to make the business perform better. Dogged by past losses when they contemplated the promotion, they gave too much weight to the effect on sales and profits of the greater sales volumes that they expected to result from their free offer. Instead of asking what could go wrong, they reached for the Upside. By doing so, they and their firm suffered very large Regret.

Whenever firms create incentive schemes or seek ways to make parts of their operations do better, they probably expose themselves to hidden risks. Maytag failed to consider that its reasonable pressure might cause risky behavior by Hoover. Plenty of banks have discovered that traders will do crazy things if they think that their bonus will be made secure by a big payoff. And plenty of firms face risks that they are often unaware of as they try to make sales staff more effective.

This last point can be illustrated by a telling example. A friend of one of the authors once came home grinning from ear to ear. Asked why, he replied that he had just had an amazing experience. He had visited a car dealer hoping to find out the price of a new model of Jeep that he wished to buy as a replacement for his current vehicle. An unusually pleasant salesman had offered him a deal that was simply too good to refuse: if he signed that day, he could trade in his old car for the new one, in effect buying the new model at a bargain price. Bowled over, he signed. And, unlike most such deals, this one turned out to be the genuine thing—the shining Jeep was acquired almost for nothing.

Was this mere luck? Had he come across a salesman who was leaving that day and wanted to harm his employer? It turned out that luck was involved, but the salesman had no ill-will toward his firm. Rather, he was working under an incentive scheme that occasionally gave him an urgent need to sell one more car. The day our friend turned up was the final day in a period of three months during which the salesman would earn a big bonus for meeting a predefined target. He was one vehicle away from meeting the target. He therefore had so much to gain from that one sale that he did not care if he virtually gave the car away—which is almost what he did.

If the deal was a win–win contract for the salesman and our friend, it was certainly not a good thing for the car dealer as a whole. The dealer "lost" the profit it would otherwise have made from a customer who was inherently likely to trade up at some point in the future. There is a message here for businesses in general. A better incentive scheme should consider that, as sales targets are approached, staff might be inclined to throw caution to the winds. By making targets more sophisticated—for instance, number of cars sold, weighted by the average margin at which they were sold—the Jeep dealer could avoid such losses in the future. Employees' desire for Upside must always be kept in balance with the firm's need for profits.

More generally, it always pays to ask whether we might inadvertently have given someone a motive to act in ways that are against our interests. The Jeep salesman's boss needed to rethink an otherwise sound compensation plan. How many managers should examine schemes that supposedly give staff incentives but in reality lead to bad decisions? Think back to our earlier analysis of mutual funds. That industry's structural problem is that fund managers have incentives that lead to bad decisions on behalf of investors.

This point reminds us of the concept of implied views. In some situations, our counterparty will be obviously desperate to do a deal with us, even if the deal looks outrageously and suspiciously cheap. Perhaps the deal is genuinely win–win. Another, perhaps more common, explanation is that some perverse incentive is causing our counterparty to offer terms that would be crazy from another perspective. In such cases, there is a danger that a win–lose contract lurks underneath the surface. But provided we think the contract will be honored (and this can be a big risk!), we have little to lose by signing. Still, we had better be sure that the "lose" element of the contract is not in fact attached to us!

The simple terms we have introduced for describing risk have broad applications when they are combined into a common language. They work with precision in technical situations, when we must weigh up two clear alternatives that offer specific payoffs for specific risks. But they also work as a framework for shaping how we think about less precise decisions in life and business. For the Upside we are being offered, what is the downside in the context of our appetite for risk? Does this deal or decision make sense on a risk-adjusted basis, so that we can be confident we are entering a win–win contract? Have we thought of scenarios under which our apparent win–win contract could turn out to be win–lose?

In sum, it seems reasonable to suggest that people should enter into deals only if they perceive the result to be win–win on a risk-adjusted basis. Each person's risk-adjusted value will depend on:

1. The scenarios being considered, which determine the calculation of Upside (U) and Regret (R).
2. The degree of risk aversion (lambda), which is context-dependent.

In negotiating a deal, one can affect the risk-adjusted value of one's counterparty by altering the perceived scenario set, biasing it either up or down. Alternatively, one can alter the payoffs. In the end, the art of deal making is to find the minimum payoffs that will give one's counterparty a positive risk-adjusted value and cause them to sign.

Chapter 9

MAKING GOOD
THINGS BETTER

Once we begin to try to manage risk, it is as if we accept a responsibility to ourselves, whether we are wearing a personal or a corporate hat. At a simple level, this means trying to think about decisions in ways that capture more of the nuances of everyday life. Using Upside and Regret, we can bring some rigor to our approach to even the most intractable of dilemmas.

But the responsibility we assume goes deeper. We can quite correctly couch many of our risk questions in terms of "Should I buy this or that?" But if we are to be true risk managers, it also follows that we should ask: "How can I remake what I have today in order to realize the best risk-adjusted returns in the future?" This captures the reality that we always have a starting position when we make a decision. Even if, as in the example that opened Chapter 5, we gain a $5,000 windfall, our starting point for deciding what to do with the money is that we now have $5,000 in addition to our existing assets and liabilities. Typically, we do not hold that money in isolation.

The logic of trying to improve what we have today is powerful. Later in this chapter, we will suggest some societal implications. But let's concentrate first on what it means for individuals. Thanks to the difficulty of measuring performance and the propaganda of the mutual funds industry, it is tricky for most people to gain an overall view of their portfolios. It is even harder for most of us to quantify in any way our overall financial health. Simply consolidating all the relevant information would be beyond most people's ability.

225

Imagine, however, that we could see a picture of our net wealth that showed its risk-adjusted characteristics and how they matched our life-long investment needs. Our first observation might be that the picture is shocking. No doubt thousands of us would be horrified to realize that we hold some quite inappropriate assets here and there. Thousands of others might see for the first time that they have systematically mismanaged their wealth. As we pointed out at the end of Chapter 4, if we are really to have sensible portfolios, then we have to understand how the different elements interact with each other. This is known as covariance, a central idea in modern finance.

Viewing our wealth in this new way, we might quickly realize something else. By changing the elements of the portfolio, or adding new elements, we could tweak our picture so that it better matches our ideal image. To recall Chapter 7, we would be seeking the best risk-adjusted portfolio for our needs and our risk appetite.

This is also one of the central ideas in modern finance. Harry Markowitz, whose work on portfolio theory won him a Nobel prize and the just tag of "father of modern finance," was among the first people to realize the intimate linkages between risk and reward. Among his insights was the notion that any portfolio can be compared to an optimal portfolio that is perfectly balanced between risk and reward. To earn a certain level of return, we must accept a consequent level of risk. However, it is possible to take more risk than is necessary to earn the same return. There is an "efficient frontier"—a line that describes risk-efficient portfolios that deliver the greatest bang per buck.

A goal of professional finance is to construct portfolios that are as close as possible to the efficient frontier. The idea behind the term "optimizing" is that we need to find the portfolio with minimal (read "optimal") risk for a given level of return. We try to create the optimal portfolio because it will produce the best value for our money.

By using Upside and Regret, we can see enormous potential gains from better risk management. If a single person optimizes, then the gains are small and narrow. But if thousands or even millions do it, then the gains are huge and widespread. People would suffer fewer disastrous financial shocks, which would create less need for the big government bailouts that are required by today's accidents. And a lot more personal wealth might be freed for immediate consumptive or productive use.

Imagine this observation being applied to the banking system. If a bank optimizes its portfolio, it might need less operating capital for the same book of business. A bank with $5 billion of capital could free, say, $50 million of capital while still operating with sufficient cushion to reassure regulators that it is not a threat to the banking system. The consequence would be interesting: Capital that is otherwise not available would be freed-up for productive use.

Now multiply this benefit among hundreds or thousands of banks. If banks optimized en masse, the overall effect on an economy would be huge. And because the gains come from money that is simply tied up at present, there would be no adverse impact on inflation. Banks would simply be making better use of what they have.

The same possibility applies to businesses of all kinds. Suppose firms were able to allocate capital to their operations just slightly more efficiently than they do today. Individually, the benefits would be small, though not insignificant. Across industry as a whole, the effect on, say, the competitiveness of American business would be dramatic.

How does optimization work? Let's start with Figure 9.1, which shows an example of an efficient frontier. (The technical material that follows is taken from research done by one of the authors and is implemented in software by his firm Algorithmics. It may be skipped without losing the main thread of our discussion.)

First, we notice that any given portfolio has a Regret and Upside that may be represented as a dot on a graph of Regret vs. Upside. It is conceivable that, for the same level of Upside, one could find another portfolio with less Regret. In fact, there must be some portfolio whose Regret is the lowest possible for the given level of Upside. We call this an efficient portfolio, in the spirit of Markowitz.

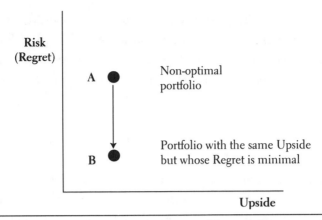

FIGURE 9.1   Optimization creating portfolios with minimal Regret.
This diagram shows 2 portfolios with different Regret but the same Upside.
The portfolios are indicated by large dots, A and B. To obtain this graph, take
your portfolio, measure its Regret and Upside, and draw it on a graph like the
one above. This would correspond to point A, because it is unlikely to be efficient. An efficient portfolio will be one that has the same Upside as your portfolio but has minimal Regret. This would correspond to portfolio B. Portfolio
B has the same Upside as yours but its Regret is the lowest possible Regret
achievable in the market under the same conditions.

There is, however, a profound difference between this idea and the
work that earned Markowitz a Nobel prize. The model we are describing is forward-looking as opposed to the historical measures Markowitz
used as inputs. The assumptions are radically different and less strin-
gent, and the portfolios we would calculate in this manner would not be
the same as his. Still, the motivation comes from his work.

By continuing the process, we could find the efficient portfolio for
any level of Upside we might choose to observe. Plotting these points
will lead to an efficient frontier, in Markowitz's terms. This is shown
in Figure 9.2.

Somewhere along the curve is the efficient portfolio that maximizes
the risk-adjusted return (Upside − λ Downside). Actually, this is easy to

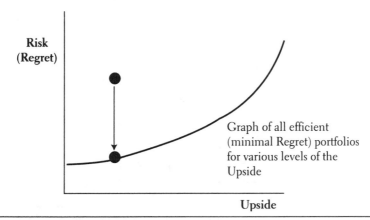

FIGURE 9.2 **Optimization creating a minimal Regret frontier.** This diagram shows where efficient portfolios are located for various levels of Upside. You can interpret it as follows. No portfolio in the market can have a lower Regret for any given level of Upside than a portfolio that would lie on the curve. All portfolios held by investors (including your own) must lie on or above the curve. The curve always has this shape because, as you seek portfolios with higher Upside, you will have to be prepared to accept more Regret. The more return you seek, the more risk you will bear. This curve is generated by a mathematical optimization problem that, for each and every level of Upside, seeks to find the portfolio in the market with minimal Regret. It is called the minimal regret (efficient frontier).

find because it can be shown mathematically that the portfolio corresponding to the point on the curve with slope = $1/\lambda$ is the portfolio that maximizes the risk-adjusted return, our ideal portfolio.

This is depicted in Figure 9.3.

This model is far easier for professional fund managers and financial engineers than for the average person, and it is no simple task even for the professionals. What concerns us, however, is that the idea can have broad-based benefits.

Think again of the banking system. The benefits from optimizing would not derive only from their ability to allocate capital more

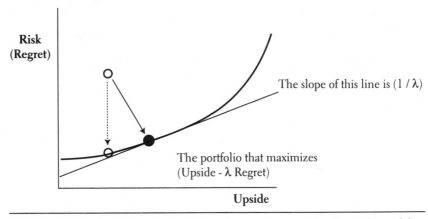

FIGURE 9.3   Optimization: Finding the maximum risk-adjusted portfolio.
This diagram shows the portfolio that is "optimal" to hold because it has maximal risk-adjusted value. Once you have generated the minimal Regret frontier, it is easy to find such a portfolio. It is the one corresponding to the point on the curve with a slope of $(1/\lambda)$.

efficiently. If they optimize their loan portfolios on a risk-adjusted basis, then they should become more stable — they would be less vulnerable to unexpected shocks from lots of loans going sour at the same time. This would dampen the volatility of the banking system and make the economy better able to withstand any changes in the environment.

Before too long, computer technology will deliver software programs that will also allow ordinary people to gain a much clearer picture of their assets and liabilities. The signs of such developments are already abundant, though few such programs have been released commercially. Several big financial firms are working on programs that will guide users through otherwise impossibly complicated investment calculations. The capacity of such programs to simplify procedures and to educate users should not be underestimated. In 1997, one small band of software rebels launched CapScape, a program designed to allow people to bypass banks when they try to raise capital for their businesses. This is not the same as giving investment advice, it is true. But the program cut the time required for creating a flotation's documentation from 900 hours to less than 20. And by obviating the need for expensive intermediaries, it makes the capital-raising process more efficient as well as faster. Programs such as this will have more and more impact as they emerge from code-writers' cubicles.

Treating People Right

Individuals will benefit in other ways. Brokers, insurers, and banks will increasingly try to help their customers to optimize their financial assets. This may seem a strange assertion. Aren't brokers more famous for churning their clients' accounts than for giving sensible risk-adjusted advice? Aren't insurers better at mis-selling investments and policies than at leading customers to well-rounded portfolios? As for banks, haven't they traditionally been bad at everything? True enough. But think of how financial services are changing as an industry and a different logic emerge.

Until perhaps a decade ago, different types of financial firms operated largely in isolation from one another. There were some grey areas; Merrill Lynch invented a brokerage account that looked like a checking account. But mostly insurers competed with each other, banks competed with banks, and brokers with brokers.

Things have changed. Even while we have been writing this book, dozens of mergers have been announced around the world that cut across once rigid industry lines. Now banks vie with brokers and insurers to sell an array of similar investment and insurance products. Although there are some remaining regulations that limit competition, these cause more nuisance than real disruption. Financial services is increasingly becoming a single industry.

This is where the optimizing effect comes from. When brokers were merely brokers, they sourced products (shares and bonds) and tried to sell them to customers in return for a fat commission. When insurance agents only sold insurance, they shamelessly steered customers toward policies that gave them the best commissions. They didn't really care if they were condemning them to earn lousy returns.

Often, consumers themselves assist in their own exploitation. Peter Carroll, a consultant with Oliver, Wyman & Company in New York, likes to point out that several groups of customers generate significant earnings for financial service providers, despite the existence of more attractive alternative services:

- Home-owning credit card customers who maintain a balance and pay non-tax-deductible interest.
- Purchasers of mutual funds that charge up-front commissions.
- Buyers of many forms of life insurance.
- People who leave large balances in non-interest-bearing current accounts.
- People who "tuck a traveler's check in their drawer for a rainy day."

With the barriers between different branches of the industry breaking down, however, the same firms that once made merry have acquired a peculiar obligation to do the right thing by their customers. They still stand to benefit by selling more products and services to their customers—indeed, arguably, such cross selling should be highly cost-effective. The firm should also benefit if it can deepen its relationships with customers, who will then be less likely to leave. But, and here's the rub, for each successive service offered to an existing customer, there is an increase in the value of the existing service relationships which are being put at risk by the sale of a potentially inappropriate product. Firms will increasingly find it is in their interests to do the right thing and help their customers to optimize their finances. Carroll says: "The emerging obligation for these firms appears to be *to do what is right for each customer,* rather than simply to maximize sales. This obligation will—on some level—be a 'moral' or 'ethical' one. In the future, it could easily come to be codified as a 'legal' one."

There is no accounting for everyone's tastes. For some people, the peace of mind represented by $200 worth of travelers' checks moldering in a desk drawer more than compensates for the lost interest on their money. For others, the 18.9 percent interest paid on a credit card balance, though not tax-deductible, may be less psychologically onerous than feeling that their home could be forfeited under a home equity line of credit. Perhaps buying a high-cost mutual fund through a known investment adviser is the equivalent of using a personal shopper at Prada to choose a dress instead of shopping in Sears or J.C. Penney. However, in time, there will be more and more pressure on the firms that sell these products to change their habits. They will be increasingly reluctant to sell things that are patently not "right" for the majority of their customers. And this should create a powerful trend toward optimization.

That is the good news. The bad news is that we should not hold our breath in readiness for a helter-skelter rush toward some financial and economic nirvana. As with past changes in finance, the big institutions will reap the early benefits and take the early risks; arguably, some are already doing so. Many years will pass before we routinely expect "optimal" advice from intermediaries and can require "optimal" decision making of ourselves. But the trend is clear. And it is based on all of the building blocks we have outlined in this book.

Reining in Banks

Everywhere we look, we can find social and business arrangements that could be improved by using a better risk-management framework. Formal optimizing is mostly the stuff of high finance; gains elsewhere tend to be fuzzy. But we can suggest some ways in which the idea of optimizing might help.

Since the 1980s, there have been big changes in the rules that govern banks. Successive banking crises led to international efforts to make banks put aside capital when they lend money or trade in markets. Agreements such as the Basle Accord set new rules for lending in 1988, and much breath was expended in the negotiations that produced them. Subsequent rules are gradually coming into force for the price risks that we described in Chapter 8.

Some of these rules are stupid. For example, the lending rules require banks to put aside capital equivalent to 8 percent of a loan they make to a corporation. It does not matter whether the corporation is a globally respected and financially solid giant or a struggling minnow: The capital charge is the same. Daft, right? Banks therefore have no capital incentive to lend sensibly (though of course they have other incentives!). The price risk rules are also riddled with problems. Many of them dictate how the overall riskiness of a bank's activities should be measured.

We hope we have shown that the problem of measuring risk of any kind is complex. There is often more than one solution. In the future, however, our risk management framework could be used to change the very basis of regulation for financial institutions. Take the simple problem of how such firms should be regulated. Should banks be treated differently from investment banks, even though these firms do many of the same things? Or should we look at the firms' functions and make rules according to what they actually do?

We suggest that these questions will eventually become largely academic. Instead, under certain ordained scenarios, financial firms of all kinds might be required by a central authority (such as a central bank or financial regulator) to account daily for the amount of Regret in their portfolios. (Alternatively, and more liberally, firms would have to show the scenarios they had used in calculating their Regret.) The

Regret number would then form the basis of a centralized insurance scheme. The regulator would sell each firm an option that protected it against its Regret, ensuring on a daily basis that there was no scope for failure. The premiums charged for the options would generate a central risk fund that could be used to compensate firms that suffered unexpected extreme negative outcomes, thereby conferring much greater stability on the financial system. This system would, in effect, create a risk tax that would protect society against the ill effects of an unlucky or a consistently poorly managed firm. Importantly, it would also act as an early-warning system because a firm that began to take lots of risk would attract higher and higher option premiums, just as an overexposed trader often faces growing margin calls. This could stop a rogue firm before it had done much damage to anyone except itself. The system would not discourage risk-taking behavior. Rather, it would ensure that risk was undertaken in more considered fashion because institutions would have to buy insurance rather than rely purely on self-insurance.

This proposed system would go a long way toward more optimal regulation. Rules would exist not for rules' sake but as protection against extreme losses. And they would encourage better behavior by the individual constituents of the market, thereby promoting greater efficiency. We will not see such a system tomorrow or in five years' time. But the related ideas of Regret, benchmarks, and optimization create a powerful toolkit with which the system can be rebuilt.

Chapter 10

KNOW YOUR RISK

He probably does not know it consciously, but Scott Adams, creator of the globally-famous cartoon character "Dilbert," is a risk-management hero. The reason? Like some others we have mentioned, Adams instinctively believes in the ideas of Upside and Regret. And by his actions, he is thoroughly endorsing the ideas of lambda and benchmarks.

We know this because Adams is someone whose ability to command material goods has been greatly altered by his success as a cartoonist, but whose views of risk have remained fundamentally sound. While a cubicle-imprisoned drone at Bell Pacific, the huge and bureaucratic American telephone firm, Adams began to draw wicked portraits of life in the modern office. In Dilbert, he captures the feelings and frustrations of a generation of workers who are baffled and terrified by the combined effects of technological change and management fads. The impact of downsizing and computers; the follies of time management, team leaders, and cubicles—all have been mocked and rocked by Dilbert's wicked humor. Perhaps the most famous Dilbert strip shows the bewildered boss complaining that his laptop computer does not work. As the boss exits, two workers ask each other whether he will ever realize that they have given him an Etch-a-Sketch.

Thanks to the success of Dilbert, Adams enjoys newfound comfort. He has changed his benchmark for cars: He traded in a Nissan for a fancy BMW. But it has not altered his enthusiasm for an intriguing idea: creating the perfect food. Here is how Adams described the idea to *The New York Times*. Imagine you could create a burrito that was entirely healthy. People who ate the burritos would feel better and would want to eat more of them. As word spread, more people might think more about their health and eat a little better, even if that only meant munching a healthy burrito instead of a fat-laden one.

But let's be optimistic. Suppose the idea really caught on and, as a result, the health of Americans improved by as little as 5 percent. The consequent reduction in healthcare and medical costs would be massive — billions of dollars would be freed for people to improve their standard of living. As Adams says, "I love anything that has no downside and potential gigantic Upside."

It should be obvious that Scott Adams has hit on our very ideas. It is not strictly true to say that his perfect-food idea has no downside: An investment is required, and it would take a big marketing effort to popularize the "Dilbert burrito." But on a risk-adjusted basis, the Upside from his scheme makes it hugely appealing. Its rationale is similar to programs designed to prevent disease: The cost of vaccines is much smaller than the cost of treating someone who has become sick. It is worth noting, too, that Adams implicitly understands the idea of optimizing. In this case, a small improvement in everyone's health can create disproportionately large benefits. Finally, now that Adams has money to play with, he can afford greater Regret, so his risk-adjusted view of the world has shifted. If only we had a *Dilbert Guide to Investing in Mutual Funds*, we might conclude that Adams has left nothing for us to say about risk!

Throughout this book, we have seen examples of ways in which people are struggling to find a language that allows a systematic and reasoned approach to risk but does not abandon the intuitions and fears that we feel in our gut. Whether for Alan Greenspan or Scott Adams, we hope that we have gone a long way toward codifying such a language, and that, from that language, we can derive a simple set of rules for managing risk. Even if too formulaic for some tastes, the rules should at least offer a beginning for better risk management. The very act of trying to "see tomorrow" should improve the decisions we make, if only because we are less likely to be surprised by unexpected outcomes.

We know that we will never be able fully to see tomorrow. Indeed, we would not like to create an impression that we are offering a risk panacea for anyone careful enough to make a few calculations. As we have said, risk is an extremely subtle and complex idea, full of fascinating byways and confusing cul-de-sacs. It defies easy capture because it can change across so many dimensions. But we owe it to ourselves to make the attempt. The more we look and the harder we think, the more we can avoid or eliminate things that would hurt us too much. Whether we are politicians, business leaders, investors, or just plain individuals, we can all do better if we seek to take control of risk.

Our starting point is simply to observe that risk is the result of the uncertainty we face in the future. Useful measures of risk should therefore look forward, not backward, in time. To the extent that history plays a role in risk measures, it defines reasonable scenarios for future events. Mostly, our future follows smoothly from our past. It is not often (although it does occur) that tomorrow's environment will be radically different from today's. Typically, one day follows the next with incremental changes in the environment. Thus, in all but totally chaotic systems, the past can be a guide to the future. But we must use such guidance with great care. The further ahead we go, the more likely that we will find larger and larger deviations from past events. Occasionally, there is a shock to our system—a market crash, an earthquake, chaos in the financial system, and so on. Risk management enables us to deal with both the typical and the unusual events.

By definition, unusual events are difficult to predict using information derived exclusively from the past. Proper measures of risk should account for both typical and atypical situations. But just how far should we go? Should we consider the possibility of the stock market's going to zero value? Should we assume that it is possible for three earthquakes a day to hit Tokyo during the next ten days? Where do we draw the line between atypical and unbelievable? A framework for risk measurement must be able to accommodate an enormous diversity of opinions about the future. No one person can have the imagination or experience to see everything that could happen. The framework must be able to deal with the past as a guide to the typical. It must include subjective assessments of the sort that we make all the time. It must be general enough to be able to handle a multitude of risks. And it must be able to present many different measures of risk, each of which might be suitable for a different situation.

To define such a framework, we need a definition of financial risk:

> Financial risk is a measure of the potential changes in value that will be experienced in a portfolio as a result of differences in the environment between now and some future point in time.

An essential prerequisite for risk measurement is our ability to determine the value of our position today. If we are unable to value correctly our holdings today, we will be unable to measure the change from today's value that the future could bring, given our chosen scenarios. As a consequence, we will be unable to measure our risk. This determining of present value is known as "marking our position to market."

Rule 1: Know the value of your holdings today.

Because the risk we assume will depend on how far in the future we wish to look, choosing the horizon over which risk is to be measured is essential for computing a value for risk. Different situations lead to different time horizons. For example, compared to a trader, a pension plan manager must control risk over much longer periods. When we think about our individual financial goals, we may have a series of scheduled objectives that will determine how far ahead we look at any given moment. For instance, while we are saving for our retirement in a decade's time, we might also need to buy a new car tomorrow.

Rule 2: Pick an appropriate future time horizon.

Risk will depend on the possible events we describe for tomorrow. These should accommodate many types of forecast—estimates based on history, subjective estimates, and estimates based on models. Probably the most general way to describe risk is to use scenarios. Each scenario leads to a future value for the portfolio under consideration. The appropriate collection of scenarios captures the likely variation in the parameters that could occur between now and the time horizon we have chosen. As we have seen, scenarios are extremely general in nature. If they are aptly chosen, they can capture all the richness we need.

Any omission of important possible events will lead to poor risk measures. Placing too heavy an emphasis on extremes may also lead to erroneous conclusions. That is why choosing scenarios is akin to the art of risk management. There are many mechanical techniques that will guide the choice of scenarios. These methods are usually good at generating the more typical events. There is a fine line between extreme, atypical situations that have value in decisions made today, and events that could not conceivably occur. The proper choice of extreme scenarios separates artists from technicians. This leads us to the third rule of risk measurement.

Rule 3: Choose a wide range of scenarios to describe possible future events; include extremes and scenarios that contradict popular opinion; include scenarios with negative outcomes that would cause Regret; assign a likelihood to each scenario.

At the very least, after scenarios have been chosen and the horizon has been determined, we will need to value our holdings under each scenario at the horizon. This will give a range of possible values that the portfolio might assume in the future.

In most situations, risk is not an absolute measure. It is invariably the risk of one action versus some other action, or the risk of one portfolio as compared with some other portfolio. For example, the risk might involve buying a stock versus keeping a portfolio unchanged. The risks to be measured would be not only the risk of holding the stock alone but also of holding the stock plus the original portfolio versus holding the original portfolio. In this case, the original portfolio is the benchmark. This is important because the future of the original portfolio as well as of the single stock will depend on the chosen scenarios. The incremental risk of holding the stock in addition to the portfolio will be different from the risk of holding the stock alone.

You can always compute the absolute risk of a portfolio by making the benchmark null (that is, setting it to zero). This brings us to the fourth rule of risk measurement.

Rule 4: Pick a benchmark.

We are now in a position to quantify risk. And here is the really amazing thing about our approach to risk: once our scenarios and benchmark have been determined, all that is left are calculations that are mechanical in nature. We have done what we can to reduce uncertainty as far as is humanly possible.

Rule 5: Value your portfolio and benchmark at the horizon under each and every future scenario.

We refer to this as Marking-to-Future. Marking-to-Market results in a unique number because there is no uncertainty; the number is today's value. Marking-to-Future results in an array of possible numbers, one for each uncertain event at that point in the future.

We can choose whatever risk measure we like. One of our central points about risk is that it means different things to different people and institutions. Different measures are applicable to the many consumers of financial risk information. A fund manager might be wholly unmoved by statistics that would be extremely useful to a bank regulator. Yet risk management has one remarkable aspect: the raw numbers that go into these different risk measures are always the same! They are always obtained from a valuation of the portfolio and benchmark under all scenarios. The measures come in many disguises but, at the end of the day, they are all derived after Rule 5 is applied either implicitly or explicitly.

Our risk measurement framework can be applied with many different risk measures, but the one that is appropriate is always context-dependent. This leads to the sixth rule of risk measurement.

Rule 6: Compute the appropriate risk measure based on values obtained by applying Rule 5.

In this framework, all risk measures are computed from the same underlying information—the values of the portfolio and benchmark at the horizon under all possible scenarios. The risk measures themselves become simply different statistics computed on the calculated data. A Value-at-Risk (VaR) number is one such statistical measure (and one that we have argued should be used with care). The standard deviation, or volatility as it is sometimes called, is another. Regret is a third. Best-case and worst-case measures generally ignore the tiny probabilities involved, but they are still simple statistics at the extreme points on the distribution of outcomes. Without doubt, other new measures that are relevant to specific categories of investors or institutions will appear in the future.

The measure we prefer, because we believe it most accurately captures the true cost of risk, is Regret—the absolute loss relative to the chosen benchmark under each scenario. Regret is positive when, if the scenario in question were to occur, you would Regret having invested in your portfolio. To measure Regret:

1. Compute the difference in the horizon values between the portfolio and the benchmark under each scenario.

2. Regret is zero whenever this number is positive. We should feel happy about our portfolio in this case.

3. Regret is the absolute value of the difference, whenever this value is negative.

4. Average Regret is the probability-weighted sum of the Regrets under each scenario.

As we have seen, there are many useful ways of applying Regret. We have argued that Regret is exactly what an insurer would have to pay you if the downside on your portfolio had been insured relative to the benchmark. Note that the insurer pays nothing if your portfolio outperforms the benchmark, and pays the absolute value of the difference if it underperforms the benchmark. Thus, the true value of this Regret is the price you would have to pay for such insurance today. We can foresee that insurance, in the future, might explicitly provide protection against Regret, something that could change financial markets in fundamental ways.

Because Regret, properly priced as insurance, is exactly the cost of eliminating all downside risk with respect to a benchmark, and because the benchmark can be arbitrary, Regret can properly be used as a comparative measure, which is not possible for other risk measures such as VaR. For the value of Regret, you can eliminate risk entirely. Regret is therefore an appropriate measure for allocating your capital among businesses (or, if you are an individual, allocating your money among investments). We regard Regret as a "perfect" measure of risk.

Our risk rules are important because they separate the process of risk management into distinct and logical steps. The choice of scenarios is separate from the choice of methodology for valuation, which is in turn separate from the particular choice of risk measure. By understanding this separateness, it is easy to compare risk measures. It is also easy to know when a particular risk measure is relevant.

As we have seen, combining Regret with Upside and then factoring in our appetite for risk (using a measure such as lambda) creates a powerful new way of approaching decisions. In many instances, we will make better decisions because we will think more clearly about the array of outcomes that could happen in the future. We can use scenarios to describe that array. And, as we have seen, simply by adopting the right benchmark, we can change the way we think about many problems.

We will never eliminate Regret. It is in the nature of things that bad, occasionally terrible, events happen that change our lives forever. Managers do make bad bets that ruin their careers. We might buy too much of an investment that later collapses and ruins us. Plenty of us get our fingers burned in the housing market because we put too little weight on Regret.

But we can use Regret against itself. If we know our potential Regret, we can avoid situations in which we are exposed. Or, we can minimize our Regret by insuring against it. Where there are efficient markets, we can do this relatively cheaply. But sometimes we will pay whatever it takes to obtain peace of mind, to the extent that we might walk away from a deal entirely. It is this impulse that must dominate our thinking about risk.

Afterword

HOW REGRET CAN
CHANGE YOUR LIFE

In late 1994, one of the authors made a disastrous decision that has caused him immense Regret. Over the stated objections of his wife and the skepticism of other family members, he sold a house in Britain, intending to avoid the property market while he was posted in New York for a few years.

With what he thought was impeccable logic, he analyzed the decision as follows. House prices had stabilized after a steep decline in the early 1990s, and they showed no sign of upward movement. The British economy was growing slowly but unspectacularly. At best, house prices might be stable, but there was, the author believed, no chance that they would rise sharply. People had absorbed the lessons of the 1980s "bubble" and were unlikely to chase prices much higher. Equally, there seemed little prospect of a sharp fall in prices, given that houses had not even returned to the levels seen during the late 1980s. Moreover, because the rent he could obtain on the house was less than the mortgage required to keep it, there would be a short-term cost that would be difficult to justify from New York, an expensive city. Better to sell the house and place the small amount of equity from it in a fixed-rate account. The house was duly (and quickly) sold.

During 1995 and the first half of 1996, there was little reason to Regret this decision; house prices were indeed going nowhere fast. Thereafter, however, the market took off with a vengeance. As middle-class families chased houses in the catchment areas of good state schools, they exposed a limited supply of large houses and a dearth of sellers in the town in question. Families in London discovered the town as a

251

pleasant place to live and a tolerable commute. They created a new category of demand and, crucially, one with plenty of ready cash on hand to bid up prices.

Prices rose in leaps and bounds. By late 1997, a house that was previously, say, £100,000 would comfortably have fetched £170,000—a whopping increase that would have been pure equity had the author only owned it! Indeed, the family's original equity stake would have quadrupled had the house sold for around that price. By this stage, the Regret caused by the original decision to sell had become enormous. Indeed, the "loss" of that equity had become the factor that constrained the author's family from buying back into the market. Prices had simply run too far ahead of his ability to pay.

Looking back on the decision, hindsight makes it easy to be wise. Indeed, a certain psychological pain is attached to that hindsight wisdom. After eighteen months, it did not seem that a big mistake had been made. A year further on, the picture had entirely changed.

What strikes the author now, however, is how a bad decision might have been avoided by better analysis. The ideas in this book could have provided the tools.

For instance, what time horizon did the author use? When making the original decision, he fixed on the immediate months after moving abroad. He gave much weight to the negative impact of the small monthly payments that would be necessary to fund the house in Britain in the event that it was rented to tenants. Arguably, the correct time horizon was several years hence, when he and his family might return to Britain and need to live in a house once again. At that point, they might benefit from having been continually exposed to the market, because they would have fared as well or as badly as everyone else. There would be no inherent disadvantage.

Second, the author was guilty of dreadful scenario planning. He dismissed the idea that prices might rise sharply, and he thereby failed to consider what missing out on a big rise might mean in the future. He focused instead on the single forecast that house prices would be largely unchanged, an assumption that proved utterly wrong. Like Paul Reichmann in Mexico, he unknowingly entered into a huge gamble while believing that he was in fact being sensible.

This combination of an incorrect time horizon and a single scenario was fatal. But the author might still have avoided disaster had he understood the idea of Regret. Indeed, he might have overcome the two other failings because Regret would have helped him to think through the issue better.

In this case, his real Regret came not from a short-term cost but from the long-term deficit caused by being out of the market. The loss of the equity he would have made, had only he kept the house, meant that he could not afford to reenter the market at the same level or higher—a Regret that was massive by comparison. Just weigh it up. It would have cost, say, £250 each month to subsidize keeping the house. Over three years, then, the author's maximum downside was £9,000 plus any decline in house prices. But the Upside (which the author did not even grace with a tiny probability, choosing instead to ignore it!) was potentially huge. In the final tally, it was more than seven times greater than the potential downside. As the author's wife now ruefully exclaims, "Where else in life can one earn this much simply by sitting tight?!"

Unwittingly, then, the author in question has learned the hard way that bad financial decisions can cause enormous Regret. His only consolation is that he now has a way to think through problems, which should help him to minimize future Regret. Other people facing similar dilemmas might take the same comfort from the ideas and rules suggested in this book.

INDEX